AF485704

This book is dedicated to our Parents:

Shree Atanu Kumar Bhaduri and Shrimati Saswati Bhaduri

– Ankan Bhaduri

Shree Nandagopal Das and Shrimati Sefali Das

– Dr. Anirban Das

Contents

Prelude

The term "Vedic" or "ancient Bharat" refers to the time in the Indian subcontinent's past when the Vedic civilisation was at its height and helped establish the social, cultural, and religious norms that still influence India today. The word "Vedic" comes from the Vedas, a body of ancient manuscripts regarded as Sanatan Hinduism's earliest holy writings.

The Vedic period traditionally mentions 64 subjects or forms of art [kalas] and 14 vidyas such as that were taught in Gurukuls, Acharyakulam and Rishikulams. These included a diverse range of subjects such as music, dance, philosophy, warfare, and sciences. The goal was to provide a complete holistic education encompassing various aspects of life and knowledge.

During the Vedic era, there was a notable eagerness for knowledge among the populace, with a strong emphasis on exploring the intricacies of existence, spirituality, and the universe. Society highly valued the oral transmission of knowledge, and the Vedic texts, encompassing hymns, rituals, and philosophical dialogues, mirrored the intellectual and spiritual aspirations prevalent during that period.

Rishis, or scholars, played a pivotal role in disseminating knowledge within gurukuls, ancient centers of education. The pursuit of knowledge was esteemed as a noble and sacred undertaking, fostering a profound exchange of ideas and wisdom. This emphasis on both spiritual and worldly knowledge significantly contributed to the intricate intellectual and cultural legacy of the Vedic era.

The text not only contains the Vedic period but also covers the post Vedic era up to 1000 CE.

During the period from 1500 BCE to 1000 CE in Bharat, there were significant developments in the fields of Mathematics, Science, Astronomy, Yoga, Literature, and Architecture.

The Vedic era began approximately 1500 BCE and lasted until 500 BCE.

A considerable deal of intellectual and cultural progress was made in ancient Bharat. On a variety of topics, including mathematics, astronomy, philosophy, medicine, and literature, scholars and sages wrote outstanding books. Scholars like Aryabhata, Charaka, and Patanjali made important advancements in their professions through their works.

There are a few incredible architectural works like, temples, caves, and monasteries are just a few of the spectacular constructions that make up ancient Bharat's architectural history. The rock-cut caverns of Ajanta and Ellora, the temples of Pattadakal and Sanchi Stupa are to name a few.

Ancient Bharat and the Vedic era have left their mark on modern Indian society. This time period is where many philosophical ideas, social institutions, and cultural and religious practises originated. The rediscovery and study of Vedic texts and ancient Bharat have played a crucial role in understanding and preserving the rich heritage of India and its enduring traditions.

This book uncovers the glorious contributions of Bharat's Mathematics, Science, Astronomy, Yoga, Literature, and Architecture reflected into thirty chapters. Chapter 1 to 10 covers the significant contributions of Piṅgala, Baudhāyana, Aryabhatta, Varāhamihira, Brahmagupta, Bhāskara I, Kātyāyana, Apastamba, Manava and Mahāvīra. Chapter 11 to 18 describes the discoveries in Science, Yoga and Astronomy by Aryabhatta, Varāhamihira, Kaṇāda, Brahmagupta, Nagarjuna, Sushruta, Charaka and Patanjali. Chapter 19 to 26 covers the works on Literature of Kālidāsa, Shudraka, Vishakhadatta, Bhavabhūti, Harisena, Bhāsa, Bāṇabhaṭṭa, and Bharavi. Chapter 27 to 30 focuses on architectural constructions made in Vedic and ancient Bharat namely Ajanta & Ellora Caves, Sanchi Stupa and Pattadakal monuments.

Swami Rwitananda Saraswati Maharaja
Adhyaksh- Kashipur Arya Samaj Gurukul
Rashtreeya Saha Adhyaksh, ALAKH AKHIL
RASHHTREEYA SANATANEE SAMSAD

Acknowledgement

I would like to extend my sincere gratitude to all the people who contributed to the creation of this book. I want to express my heartfelt gratitude to my parents, teachers and importantly Professor Anirban Das in particular for their continuous support, wisdom, and inspiration during this journey.

My parents, Shree Atanu Kumar Bhaduri and Shrimati Saswati Bhaduri have always been my source of support and love. My teachers, Sir Arvind Pathak and Sir Pankaj Rathore supported me at every point. I cannot forget the motivation that I got from Professor Anirban Das, without him this book would remain incomplete. My achievements have been motivated by their support and unshakable faith in me, and I am incredibly grateful for their blessings.

I convey a debt of deep sense of respect to my teachers who have fostered my zeal for studying and shared their skills and knowledge with me. Without the combined efforts and encouragement of everyone named above, this book would not have been possible, and for that,

I will always be grateful.

– Ankan Bhaduri

I sincerely put across the heartiest homage to my research guide, Late Prof. Dr. Kajla Basu, Hon'ble Head of the Department, Department of Mathematics, National Institute of Technology, Durgapur, West Bengal.

I put across homage from the bottomless depth of my heart to Prof. (Dr) Dilip Kr. Banerjee, Former Pro Vice Chancellor, Central University of Jharkhand whose blessings uncovered our latent potential that made this book into a successful endeavor.

I convey our profound gratitude and deep respect to Mr Madhup Kr Roy, Hon'ble General Secretary, Haldia Cultural Forum, Haldia, West Bengal.

I express deep sense of gratitude to Prof. (Dr) GL. Sharma, Director – Sikkim Manipal Institute of Technology, Sikkim.

I am especially indebted to Dr. Samarjit Kar, Professor, Department of Mathematics, NIT Durgapur, Dr. Goutam Panigrahi, Assistant Professor, Department of Mathematics, NIT Durgapur.

I am especially indebted to Dr. Amar Kishor, hon'ble former HOD, Department of Mathematics, Amity University Kolkata.

I convey my heartfelt gratitude to Prof. Dr. Rajiv Ganguly, Dean, UEM Kolkata.

I am thankful to all my colleagues of University of Engineering and Management, Kolkata.

Love to Baishali Banerjee, Subhajit Sabui, Bodhisatwa Chatterjee and Sagar Kumar Dhawa. Your encouragement and inspirations have shaped this book. I am especially indebted to my family members: Dr Paramita Das Pattanayak, Dr Sourav Pattanayak, Somsubhra Pattanayak, Sankhasubhra Pattanayak, Prof. Anupam Das, Tusi Das, Swaralipi Das, and Swaramita Das (Delta) without whose never-ending support and unbounded eternal love, this book could not have been brought into existence.

This book was not possible without the sleepless nights spent by my coauthor, Mr. Ankan Bhaduri. Thank you Ankan for everything.

This book has been my long cherished dream, which would not have been turned into reality without the motivation and inspiration of my wife Nibedita. Love to Swaraleena (Pekhom), my daughter, who has changed the philosophy of my life.

– Dr. Anirban Das

Introduction

The term "Vedic" or "ancient Bharat" refers to the time in the Indian subcontinent's past when the Vedic civilization was at its height and helped establish the social, cultural, and religious norms that still influence India today. The term "Vedic" originates from the Vedas, a body of ancient manuscripts regarded as Hinduism's earliest holy writings. The text not only contains the Vedic period but also covers the post Vedic era up to 1000 CE.

During the period from 1500 BCE to 1000 CE in Bharat, there were significant developments in the fields of Mathematics, Science, Astronomy, Yoga, Literature, and Architecture.

The Vedic era began approximately 1500 BCE and lasted until 500 BCE.

A considerable deal of intellectual and cultural progress was made in ancient Bharat. On a variety of topics, including mathematics, astronomy, philosophy, medicine, and literature, scholars and sages wrote outstanding books. Scholars like Aryabhata, Charaka, and Patanjali made important advancements in their professions through their works.

There are a few incredible architectural works like, temples, caves, and monasteries are just a few of the spectacular constructions that make up ancient Bharat's architectural history. The rock-cut caves of Ellora and Ajanta, the temples of Pattadakal and Sanchi Stupa are to name a few.

Ancient Bharat and the Vedic era have left their mark on modern Indian society. This time period is where many philosophical ideas, social institutions, and cultural and religious practices originated. The rediscovery and study of Vedic texts and ancient Bharat have played a significant role in understanding and preserving the rich heritage of India and its enduring traditions.

This book uncovers the glorious contributions of Bharat's Mathematics, Science, Astronomy, Yoga, Literature, and Architecture reflected into thirty chapters. Chapter 1 to 10 covers the significant contributions of Piṅgala, Baudhāyana, Aryabhatta, Varāhamihira, Brahmagupta, Bhāskara I, Kātyāyana, Apastamba, Manava and Mahāvīra. Chapter 11 to 18 describes the discoveries in Science, Yoga and Astronomy by Aryabhatta, Varāhamihira, Kaṇāda, Brahmagupta, Nagarjuna, Sushruta, Charaka and Patanjali. Chapter 19 to 26 covers the works on Literature of Kālidāsa, Shudraka, Vishakhadatta, Bhavabhūti, Harisena, Bhāsa, Bāṇabhaṭṭa, and Bharavi. Chapter 27 to 30 focuses on architectural constructions made in Vedic and ancient Bharat namely Ajanta & Ellora Caves, Sanchi Stupa and Pattadakal monuments.

Section I

Mathematics

Chapter 1

Piṅgala

Introduction

In the 2nd century BCE Indian Mathematics was gifted with several combinatorics, theories, algorithms. Sanskrit was the mother language as all the mathematical formulations were designed by the legendary mathematicians. Of them, Piṅgala's theories and combinatorics had a gigantic contribution in the arena of mathematical sciences.

Fig 1.1.1: Pingala

(https://postcard.news/wp-content/uploads/2019/08/Acharya-Pingala.png)

In diversified fields of theorizing mathematical sciences, canvased in Sanskrit, Piṅgala[1] had enormous contributions like, Recursive algorithms which is considered as the first instance in Indian context, calculations on binomial coefficients, iterative partial sums of sequences, calculation of summing geometric series and many more.

Theories

Chandas, is indeed one of the six *Vedangas*, which are the auxiliary disciplines that support the study and understanding of the Vedas, the ancient sacred scriptures of India. *Chandas* specifically deals with the science of prosody or metrics in Sanskrit poetry. *Pratyayas*, which are linguistic affixes and elements in Sanskrit, hold a crucial role in the evolution and expansion of meters (*chandas*) in Sanskrit poetry. These linguistic components are instrumental in creating the intricate rhythmic and metrical patterns that define Sanskrit poetic compositions.

Within the realm of *Chandas Shastra*, the science of prosody, *Pratyayas* serve as essential tools for poets to manipulate and extend the basic metrical structures. They enable poets to modify the length of syllables, introduce pauses, and adjust stress patterns to create a diverse array of poetic meters. By adeptly using *Pratyayas*, poets can craft verses in various meters, each possessing its unique aesthetic and rhythmic characteristics.

In essence, *Pratyayas* are the building blocks that poets use to construct the diverse and captivating landscape of Sanskrit poetry, while adhering to the foundational principles and rules of *Chandas*. There are six *Pratyayas*[2] which means problems and their solutions which were identified by some Sanskrit prosodists. Nomenclature of those *Pratyayas* were not done by Piṅgala. Piṅgala's works are documented in *Chhandashastra*[3]. The six *Pratyayas* are:

Prastāra[4,5]

The term "prastāra" means permutation, used in Sanskrit Prosody (*Chanda Shastra*), which refers to a technical concept that allows calculation and creation of various poetic meters (*chandas*). It is used to list all forms of n-syllable meters with 1-syllable using G and L where G and L denotes long (Guru) and short (Laghu) respectively. We are representing Pingala's prastāra in modern binary format.

For example:

Index	Prastāra
1	G
2	L

If n = 1 then:

Similarly, if n = 2 then:

Index	Prastāra
1	GG
2	LG
3	GL
4	LL

Similarly for n = 3, n = 4 and so on

If it is observed carefully then it resembles the modern binary number system.

Index	Decimal	Prastāra	Binary number system
1.	0	GG	00
2.	1	LG	01
3.	2	GL	10
4.	3	LL	11

If it is observed carefully then Pingala's Binary System is just the mirror image of the modern Binary number system.

If G is substituted with 0 and L is substituted with 1 then we can obtain the following table:

Index	Decimal	Prastāra (G=0, L=1)	Binary Number
1	0	0	0
2	1	10	1
3	2	1	10
4	3	11	11

Naṣṭaṃ[6]

Naṣṭaṃ is a process to find the lost or corrupted row (*Nasht*). This algorithm is used to find the combination from the index.

For n= 3 Prastāra (modern format) is:

Index	Prastāra
1	GGG
2	LGG
3	GLG
4	LLG
5	GGL
6	LGL

7	GLL
8	LLL

Naṣṭaṃ algorithm:

नष्टवृत्तपरिज्ञानार्थमाह—

लर्द्धे ॥ ८ । २४ ॥

यदेवं विजिज्ञासेत—गायत्र्यां समवृत्तं मष्टं कीदृशमिति, तदा तमेव पदसङ्ख्याविशेष-मर्धयेत । तस्मिन्नर्धीकृते लघुरेको लक्ष्यते, स भूमौ विन्यास्यः ।

इदानीमवशिष्टा त्रिसंख्याविषमत्वादर्धयितुं न शक्यते । तत्र किं प्रतिपत्तव्यमित्याह—

सैके ग ॥ ८ । २५ ॥

अर्घं इत्यनुवर्तते । विषमसङ्ख्यायामेकमधिकं निक्षिप्य ततोऽर्धयेत । तत्रैको गकारो लभ्यते । तं पूर्वलब्धाल्लकारात् परं स्थापयेत् । ततो द्विसंख्यायवदिष्यते । पुनस्तामर्ध-येत, तत्रैकलकारं दद्यात् । ततश्चैकसंख्यायवदिष्यते । तत्र तावत् सैके मिति लक्षण-मावर्तनीयं यावद्वृत्ताक्षराणि षट् पूर्यन्ते । एवं सङ्ख्यान्तरेऽपि योज्यम् ॥

Pingala, Chhandashastra 8.24 and 8.25

We are representing the Naṣṭaṃ procedure in today's mathematical format:

Let us consider that the combination of index 'm' is to be identified.

The algorithm states that if 'm' is even then append L and halve it and if 'm' is odd then add 1 to 'm' and append G and halve it and continue until 'm' becomes 1.

Example: for m = 4, the combination is LLG

1. As m = 4 so 'm' is even so append L and halve 'm' so 'm' becomes 2 therefore result = L
2. As m = 2 so 'm' is even so append L and halve 'm' so 'm' becomes 1 therefore result = LL
3. As m = 1 so 'm' is odd so append G and add 1 to 'm' and halve 'm' so 'm' becomes 1 therefore result = LLG

Uddiṣṭaṃ[7]

To determine the desired (Uddiṣṭaṃ) row index without starting the count from the top row from a given prastara. This algorithm is to identify the index from the combination.

Uddiṣṭaṃ algorithm:

उद्दिष्टवृत्तस्य सङ्ख्यापरिज्ञानार्थमाह—

प्रतिलोमगणं द्विर्लाद्यम् ॥ ८ । २६ ॥

यस्य वृत्तस्य सङ्ख्यां जिज्ञासेत तद्रूपौं प्रस्तारयेत् । ततस्तस्यान्ते यो लकारः सजाती-यापेक्षया, तमादौ कृत्वा प्रतिलोम्येन द्विरावर्तयेत् । तत्र निराकाराया आवृत्तेरसम्भवात् प्रथमातिक्रमे कारणाभावादेकसङ्ख्या लभ्यते । ततश्चैकसङ्ख्याङ्कमन्त्यलकारस्याधस्तात् स्थापयित्वा द्विगुणयेत् । ततस्तस्मादपनीय तत्पूर्वस्य वर्णस्याधस्तान्निधाय पुनर्द्विगुणयेत् । पुनस्तदपि पूर्वस्य । एवं यावन्ति वृत्ताक्षराणि प्रातिलोम्येन समाप्यन्ते । तत्र याः सङ्ख्या निष्पद्यन्ते, तावतिथं तद्वृत्तमिति ॥

तत्र निक्षेपमाह—

ततोऽन्येकं जह्यात् ॥ ८ । २७ ॥

पूर्वोक्ते कर्मणि क्रियमाणे यदि सा सङ्ख्या गकारस्थानमापद्यते, तदा तां द्विगुणयित्वा ततः सङ्ख्यासमुदायादेकं त्यजेत् । ततः पूर्वोक्तं कर्म कुर्यात् । ततः परिपूर्णत्वात्तद्वृत्त-सङ्ख्या सिध्यति ॥

Pingala, Chhandashastra 8.26 and 8.27

Explanation of Uddiṣṭaṃ algorithm according to modern day mathematical format:

This algorithm states that start the value of index (m) with 1 and start scanning from right to left until the first L is encountered. As soon as the first L is found, double 'm' and continue. As the G is encountered then double the 'm' and subtract 1 from it.

Example: for combination GLG the index is 3

1. $m = 1$ GL<u>G</u>. As G is encountered and first L is not evaluated so skip and move left.

2. m = 1 GL̲G. As first L is encountered so double 'm' then 'm' becomes 2.

3. m = 2 G̲LG. As G is encountered and first L was evaluated so double 'm' and 'm' becomes 4 and subtract 1 from 'm' therefore 'm' becomes 3

Hence for combination GLG index is 3.

Lagakriyā[8]

This process is used to find k syllables from n-syllable meter. Let us describe the process to select the "k" objects from the collection of "n" objects.

For example:

If we wish to select 3 objects from a collection of 4 objects such as P, Q, R and S, then the combination of P, Q and R is the same as the combination Q, R and P. So in this way we only have 4 possible combinations and those are PQR, PQS, PRS and QRS. So we can select among these combinations.

In modern mathematics it is considered as binomial coefficients i.e. ^nC_k where "n" depicts no. of objects from which we are selecting and "k" is number of objects that is to be selected. The formula for ^nC_k is:

$$^nC_k = [(n)(n-1)(n-2)....(n-k+1)]/[(k)(k-1)(k-2).......(1)]$$

For the above example n = 4 and k = 3

$$^4C_3 = (4 \times 3 \times 2)/(3 \times 2 \times 1) = 4$$

The *sutra* that was given by Piṅgala was:

परे पूर्णम् ॥ ८ । ३४ ॥

तदेतच्छन्दोवृत्तसङ्ख्याजातं द्विगुणितं पूर्णमेव स्थापयितव्यम् , न द्वयूनम् । परे छन्दसि

परे पूर्णमिति ॥ ८ । ३५ ॥

उपरिष्टादेकं चतुरस्रकोष्ठं लिखित्वा तस्याधस्तादुभयतोऽर्धनिष्क्रान्तं कोष्ठकद्वयं लिखेत् । तस्याप्यधस्ताञ्त्रयं तस्याप्यधस्ताच्चतुष्टयं यावदभिमतं स्थानमिति मेरुप्रस्तारः ॥ तस्य प्रथमे कोष्ठे एकसंख्यां व्यवस्थाप्य लक्षणमिदं प्रवर्तयेत् । तत्र परे कोष्ठे यदुत्तरसंख्याजातं तत् पूर्वकोष्ठयोः पूर्णं निवेशयेत् । तत्रोभयोः कोष्ठकयोरेकैकमङ्कं दद्यात् , मध्ये कोष्ठे तु परको-ष्ठद्वयाङ्कमेकीकृत्य पूर्णं निवेशयेदिति पूर्णशब्दार्थ । चतुर्थ्यां पङ्क्तावपि पर्यन्तकोष्ठयोरेके-कमेव स्थापयेत् । मध्यमकोष्ठयोस्तु परकोष्ठद्वयाङ्कमेकीकृत्य पूर्णं निरङ्कारूपं स्थापयेत् । उत्तरत्राप्ययमेव न्यास. । तत्र द्विकोष्ठायां पङ्क्तौ एकाक्षरस्य विन्यासः । तत्रैकगुर्वेकलघु-वृत्तं भवति ॥ तृतीयाया पङ्क्तौ द्व्यक्षरस्य प्रस्तारः । तत्रैकं सर्वगुरु, द्वे एकलघुनी, एकं सर्वलघ्विति कोष्ठकक्रमेण वृत्तानि भवन्ति ॥ चतुर्थ्यां पङ्क्तौ त्र्यक्षरस्य प्रस्तार· । तत्रैकं सर्वगुरु त्रीण्येकलघूनि त्रीणि द्विलघूनि एकं सर्वलघु ॥ तथा पञ्चमादिपङ्क्तावपि सर्वगुर्वा-दिसर्वलघ्वन्तमेकद्व्यादिलघु द्रष्टव्यमिति ॥

Pingala, Chhandashastra 8.34 and 8.35

Pare pūrṇaṃ which means "next full". *Pare pūrṇamiti* which means "next full and so on".

Halayudha was a 10th century Sanskrit mathematician, who worked on Pingala's *Chhandashastra* and claimed that the above *sutra* is used to calculate the binomial coefficient. He also claimed that the last *sutra* refers to *meru-Prastāra* (Pascal's triangle in modern mathematical science). Then Halayudha explained the *sutra* in detail:

1. Keep a cell at the top.
2. Keep two cells below the top cell, then keep 3 cells below the above two cells and proceed until desired number is obtained.

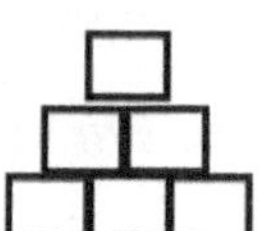

3. Keep 1 in the top cell. Then the summation of the no.s of the above two cells are put down for the below cells.

$$1 \text{ — row no. 0}$$

$$1\ 1 \text{ — row no. 1}$$

$$1\ 2\ 1 \text{ — row no. 2}$$

$$1\ 3\ 3\ 1 \text{ — row no. 3}$$

$$1\ 4\ 6\ 4\ 1 \text{ — row no. 4}$$

In modern mathematical science it is considered as Pascal's triangle.

For nth row the elements are:

$${}^{n}C_0, {}^{n}C_1, ..., {}^{n}C_n$$

Example:

For 3rd row the elements are:

$${}^{3}C_0, {}^{3}C_1, {}^{3}C_2, {}^{3}C_3$$

$${}^{3}C_0$$ is equal to 1

$${}^{3}C_1$$ is equal to 3

$${}^{3}C_2$$ is equal to 3

$${}^{3}C_3$$ is equal to 1

So the elements becomes 1,3,3,1

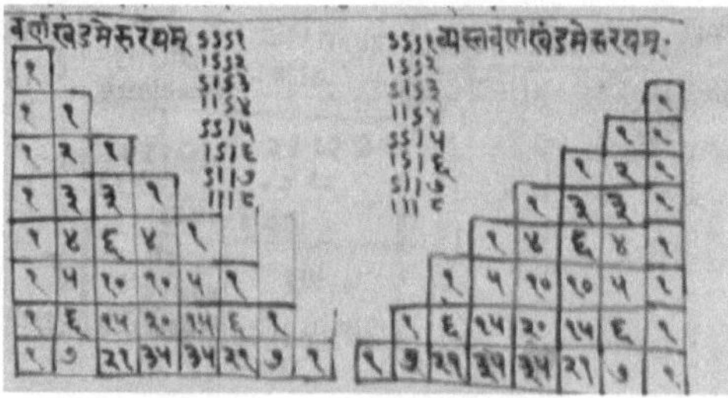

Fig 1.1.2: Meru Prastaara
(https://upload.wikimedia.org/wikipedia/commons/d/dd/Meru_
Prastaara.png)

Saṅkhyā[9]

This algorithm is used evaluate the total no. of meters possible from the given no. of syllables.

प्रस्तारादिना वृत्तसङ्ख्यापरिज्ञानार्थमाह—

द्विरर्द्धे ॥ ८ । २८ ॥

अपनीत इत्यध्याहारः । यदा जिज्ञासेत्—पडक्षरे छन्दसि कति वृत्तानि भवन्ति ? तदा ता छन्दोऽक्षरसङ्ख्यां भूमौ स्थापयित्वा ततोऽर्धमपनयेत् । तस्मिन्नपनीते द्वौ लभ्येते । ततस्ता द्विसङ्ख्यां भूमौ पृथक् प्रस्तारयेत् । तत. शेषाज्ञ्योऽक्षरसङ्ख्यायां भवन्ति ॥

तेषामर्धयितुमशक्यत्वात् किं कर्तव्यमित्याह—

रूपे शून्यम् ॥ ८ । २९ ॥

विषमसङ्ख्यातो रूपमपनीय तस्मिन्नपनीते शून्यं लभ्यते । तत्र पूर्वलब्धाया. द्वि-सङ्ख्याया अधस्तात् स्थापयेत्, ततो द्विसङ्ख्यावशिष्यते । ततोऽर्धेऽपनीते पुनर्द्विसङ्ख्या लभ्यते, तां शून्याधस्तात् स्थापयेत् । ततो रूपे शून्यं लभ्यते । तद् द्विसङ्ख्याया अध-स्तात् स्थापयेत् ॥

ततः किं कर्तव्यमित्याह—

द्विः शून्ये ॥ ८ । ३० ॥

शून्यस्थाने द्विराद्वृत्ति कुर्यात् । तत्र निराकारायाः आद्यवृत्तेरसम्भवात्, प्रथमातिक्रमे कारणाभावादेकसङ्ख्या लभ्यते । तां शून्ये स्थापयित्वा द्विगुणयेत् । ततो द्वौ . भवतः । तस्योपरिष्टादर्धस्थानं द्विसङ्ख्यार्कं तदपनीय तस्य स्थाने तं द्विसङ्ख्यार्कं स्थापयेत् ॥

अनन्तरमिदं कर्तव्यमित्याह—

तावदर्धे तद्गुणितम् ॥ ८ । ३१ ॥

यदर्धस्थाने स्थितं सङ्ख्याजातं, तत्तावत् गुणितं कुर्यात् । एतद्दुर्कं भवति—खसङ्ख्य-यैव गुणयितव्यमिति । ततो द्वौ द्वाभ्यां गुणितौ चत्वारो भवन्ति । तेषामुपरिष्टाच्छून्य-स्थानं तत्र तानारोपयेत् । अनन्तरं द्वि शून्य इति द्विगुणिता अष्टौ भवन्ति । तानप्यर्ध-

Pingala, Chhandashastra 8.28, 8.29, 8.30, 8.31

Explanation of the above algorithm is discussed in light of modern mathematics:

Sn can be calculated using following formula:-

$S_n = (2^{n/2})^2$ where n is even no. $S_n = 2.2^{(n-1)}$ where n is odd no.

For example, when n=3:

$$N = 3 \quad 2.2^{(3-1)} = 8$$

$$n = 2 \quad (2^{2/2})^2 = 4$$

$$n = 1 \quad 2.2^{(1-1)} = 2$$

Total number S_3 of length 3 is 8. Pingala states that the list of several forms of n-syllable meter includes lists of several forms of all meters with lesser syllables and demonstrates it in the form of sum of a geometric series. Pingala's *sutra* was:

द्विर्यूनं तदन्तानाम् ॥ ८ । ३२ ॥

गायत्र्यादिवृत्तसमुदायजातं द्विगुणीकृत्य द्वाभ्यामूनं कुर्यात् । तत्तदन्तानां परिमाणं भवति । यस्य छन्दसः संख्या द्विगुणिता, तत्पर्यन्तानां पूर्वेषामेकाक्षरप्रभृतीनां संख्या भवतीत्यर्थः ॥

Pingala,Chhandashastra 8.32

The above sutra according to modern mathematical format is:

$$2S_n - 2 = S_1 + S_2 + S_3 + \ldots + S_n$$

$$2.2^n - 2 = 2^1 + 2^2 + 2^3 + \ldots + 2^n$$

Where

$S_n = (2^{n/2})^2$ where n is even no. $S_n = 2.2^{(n-1)}$ where n is odd no. As shown above.

Adhva Yoga[10]

This *pratyayas* is used to measure the space required to compose the list of the different forms of meter. As per Janāśraya, each line's width corresponds to the width of a finger. He then calculated that the space needed to write the forms of the 24 syllable meter is 33,554,431 finger-widths which is approximately 265 miles.

Chapter 2

Baudhāyana

Introduction

In the previous chapter we have gone through the contribution of Piṅgala, a Sanskrit-mathematical scholar of 2nd century B.C.E. In this chapter we are going to study about another Sanskrit mathematician named Baudhāyana[11,12] (800 B.C.E – 740 B.C.E) whose contribution was gigantic in nature in terms of world of mathematical landscape. Discoveries of Baudhāyana were mainly on Geometry and evaluating the value of pi(π).

Fig 1.2.1: Baudhāyana
(https://d138zd1ktt9iqe.cloudfront.net/media/seo_landing_files/
image-001-1600667148.png)

Theories

Baudhāyana composed a book named Śulbasûtra which consists of two words Śulba which means measuring tape or cord and *sûtra* which means a rule.

Baudhāyana[13,14] in Śulbasūtra revealed several geometrical truths. Śulbasūtra consists of a theory which states that the square of hypotenuse of a rectangular triangle is the sum of square of the sides that make the right angle. Although the theorem in Śulbasūtra does not contain right angled triangle but the theorem encompasses the relationship among the sides of the squares or rectangle and the diagonal. The rule in Śulbasūtra states that:

दीर्घचतुरस्रस्याक्ष्णया रज्जुः पार्श्वमानी तिर्यग् मानी च यत् पृथग् भूते कुरूतस्तदुभयं करोति ॥ ॥[15]

The above *sutra* means that the areas produced by the diagonals of the rectangle equals areas produced by the horizontal and vertical sides of the rectangle separately. More specifically area of squares is formed by the length, breadth and diagonal of a rectangle. The area of the square formed by the diagonal equals the area of square formed by the length and the area of square formed by the breadth.

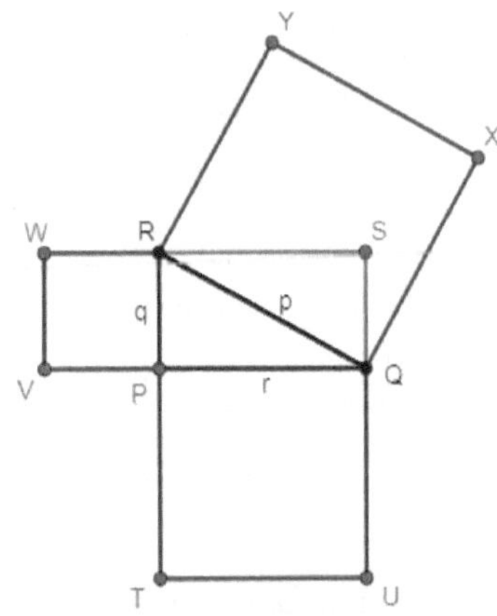

Fig 1.2.2: Pictorial representation of Baudhāyana's sutra[16].

$$q^2 + r^2 = p^2$$

There were several other discoveries[17] such as circling a square, finding the value of pi. Baudhāyana found the approximate value of pi to be 3 and found the value of root 2 to be 1.414216.

Chapter 3

Aryabhatta

Introduction

In the previous chapter we have discussed about Baudhāyana, his theories and discoveries on geometry which resembles Pythagorean Theorem and on several other sectors which he discovered in about 8th century B.C.E. In this chapter we are going to acquire knowledge about the theories and discoveries of Aryabhatta[18] which was done on around 499 A.D. The mathematical works of Aryabhatta include arithmetic, algebra, plane trigonometry as well as spherical trigonometry and on several other parts.

Fig 1.3.1: Aryabhatta
(https://upload.wikimedia.org/wikipedia/commons/a/af/2064_aryabhata-crp.jpg)

Theories

Aryabhatta revealed several mathematical truths, among them some are as follows:

Value of pi (π)[19]:

Aryabhatta calculated an approximate value of pi (π). According to his theory the value of pi (π) is:

$$\pi = \frac{62832}{20000} = 3.1416$$

As we know that the original value of pi (π) = 3.1415926536

(Calculated in calculator) as it is non-recurring non-terminating decimal so the value of never ends and he determined the value of π accurately to three decimal places. If it is observed carefully even 22/7 is also not that accurate because:

$$\pi = \frac{22}{7} = 3.142857142$$

Trigonometry:

The contribution of Aryabhatta in trigonometry[20] is gigantic because he proposed the table of sine and named it *jya*[21] which means half chord. In the history this table was first to be used as standard table in India.

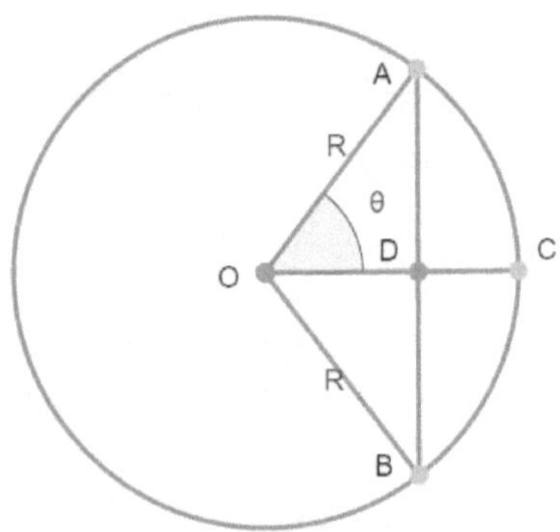

Fig 1.3.2: Image which contains jya (half chord)[22].

The radius (OA) of the above circle is R, *jya* or the half chord is AD. Let AD = S and mathematically:

$$S = R\sin(\theta), \text{ where } S = AD$$

Table of sine proposed by Aryabhatta consist of values of S for many angles taking $R = 3438$ units:

Table 1: Aryabhatta Sine table[23]

Angle (A) (in degrees, arcminutes)	Äryabhata's value of jya (A)	Modern value of jya (A) (3438 x sin (A))
03° 45'	225'	224.856
07° 30'	449'	448.749
11° 15'	671'	670.7205
15° 00'	890'	889.8199
18° 45'	1105'	1105.108
22° 30'	1315'	1315.665
26° 15'	1520'	1520.588
30° 00'	1719'	1719

33° 45'	1910'	1910.05
37° 30'	2093'	2092.921
41° 15'	2267'	2266.83
45° 00'	2431'	2431.033
48° 45'	2585'	2584.825
52° 30'	2728'	2727.548
56° 15'	2859'	2858.592
60° 00'	2978'	2977.395
63° 45'	3084'	3083.448
67° 30'	3177'	3176.297
71° 15'	3256'	3255.545
75° 00'	3321'	3320.853
78° 45'	3372'	3371.939
82° 30'	3409'	3408.587
86° 15'	3431'	3430.639
90° 00'	3438'	3438

Many more discoveries were done by Aryabhatta on the topics Arithmetic, Algebra, Spherical trigonometry and many more.

Chapter 4

Varāhamihira

Introduction

Varāhamihira[24] was an Indian mathematician, scientist, astronomer as well as astrologer. His works in astronomy was compiled by him in *Panchasiddhantika* and *Brahatsamhita*. The main contributions of Varāhamihira in the subject mathematics was in trigonometry in which there were certain formulae that was proposed by him as well as correction of the sine table which was calculated by Aryabhatta, the way to solve combination and there were several theories of numbers.

Fig 1.4.1: Varāhamihira
(https://qph.cf2.quoracdn.net/main-qimg-
400bb7779a00dca74d67a702468bdd48-lq)

Theories

There are several mathematical solutions which were discovered by Varāhamihira and some of them are:

Trigonometry:

There are several trigonometric equations those were discovered by the famous mathematician Varāhamihira and those trigonometric equations[25] are:

$$sin(x) = cos\left(\frac{\pi}{2} - x\right)$$

$$sin^2(x) + cos^2(x) = 1$$

$$\left(1 - cos(2x)\right)/2 = sin^2(x)$$

Combination(^{n}Cr):

Today the problem of the combination is solved in the following way:

$$^nCr =$$

$$n(n-1)(n-2)...(n-r+1)/r$$

$$^nCr = \frac{n!}{r!(n-r)!}$$

where

$$n! = n(n-1)\,(n-2)\,...1$$

The above problem was solved by Varāhamihira in the following way[26]:

1. Write the n of ^nC_r in a column taking n=1 at bottom:

4				
3				
2				
1				
n	1	2	3	4

2. Write the r of ^nC_r in a row taking r = 1 at left.

4				
3				
2				
1				
n/r	1	2	3	4

3. Start from the bottom left side where values of 'n' and 'r' are 1, put there 1

4				
3				
2				
1	1			
n/r	1	2	3	4

4. Calculate the value at any place provided that n >= r by summing the number below that place and the number below of its immediate left. For example:

x

z y

$x = y+z$ as y is below x and z is immediate left of y.

After following the above steps, the complete table would be:

4	4	6	4	1
3	3	3	1	
2	2	1		
1	1			
n/r	1	2	3	4

If the above table is rotated it would form the pascal's triangle.

Chapter 5

Brahmagupta

Introduction

Brahmagupta[27] (598 A.D – 660 A.D approx.) was a profound mathematician, scientist as well as astronomer. He was born in Ujjain in 598 A.D. His contribution in mathematics, physics and astronomy is huge.

His discoveries were related with arithmetic, algebra, geometry etc. in mathematics.

Fig 1.5.1: Brahmagupta
(https://d138zd1ktt9iqe.cloudfront.net/media/seo_landing_files/
image-001-1600757408.png)

Theories

Contribution of Brahmagupta in mathematics is vast. Among those theories some are stated below:

Quadratic Equation:

There were two rules[28] which were given by Brahmagupta to solve a quadratic equation:

$$a\,x^2 + bx - c = 0$$

First, he provided the formula to evaluate the above mentioned quadratic equation is:

$$x = \frac{\pm\sqrt{b^2 + 4ac} - b}{2a}$$

Then he provided his next formula:

$$x = \frac{\pm\sqrt{ac + \left(\frac{b}{2}\right)^2} - \left(\frac{b}{2}\right)}{a}$$

Series:

Brahmagupta gave the formula[29] to compute sum of

1. Series of cubes
2. Series of squares

Brahmagupta's formula for sum of squares for first n numbers is:

$$1^2 + 2^2 + 3^2 + \ldots + n^2 = \frac{n(n+1)(2n+1)}{6}$$

Brahmagupta's formula for sum of cubes for first n digits is:

$$1^3 + 2^3 + 3^3 + \ldots + n^3 = \left(\frac{n(n+1)}{2}\right)^2$$

Geometry:

Brahmagupta proposed a theorem[30] regarding quadrilateral which is one of his great discoveries. The theorem states that:

"If a cyclic quadrilateral is orthodiagonal (i.e., has perpendicular diagonals), then the perpendicular to a side from the point of intersection of the diagonals always bisects the opposite side.[31]"

The above statement means that let a cyclic and ortho-diagonal quadrilateral be PQRS where PR and QS are diagonals and both are perpendicular to each other:

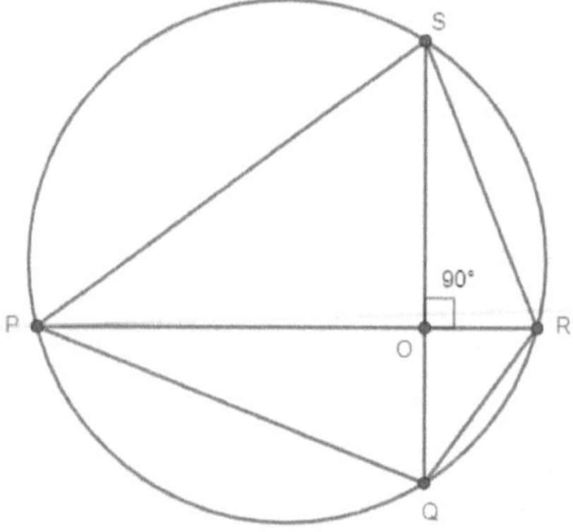

Fig 1.5.2: Pictorial representation of the Brahmagupta's theorem.[32]

Now draw a perpendicular line from O on RS and name it N as follows:

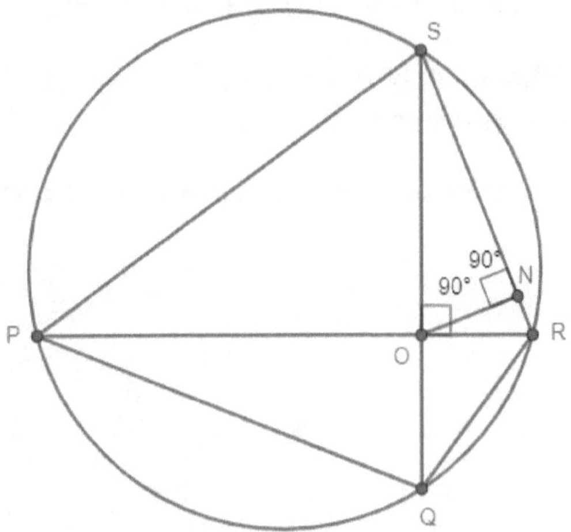

Fig 1.5.3: Pictorial representation of the Brahmagupta's theorem.[33]

Next extend the line ON backwards and let it fall on PQ and name it M as shown below:

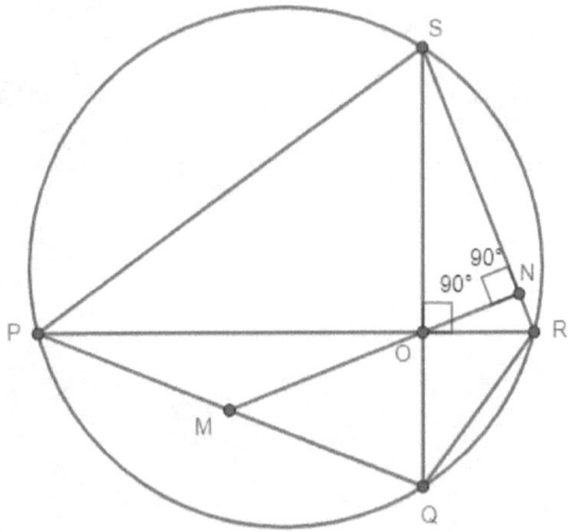

Fig 1.5.4: Pictorial representation of the Brahmagupta's theorem.[34]
Then M is the midpoint of PQ.

Some other discoveries[35,36] of Brahmagupta are:

1. Interpolation formula
2. Approximation of π

There are more mathematical discoveries of Brahmagupta.

Chapter 6

Bhāskara I

Introduction

Bhāskara I[37] was a great mathematician and astronomer of 7th century. In the name Bhāskara I the 'I' was given just to differentiate him with a 12th century mathematician and astronomer Bhāskaracharya. Bhāskara I is known for his exceptional and remarkable work in trigonometry where he approximated the sine function with an accuracy of about 99%.

Fig 1.6.1: Bhāskara I
(https://www.booksfact.com/images/science/ancient_science/
bhaskaracharya.jpg)

Theories

The main discovery of Bhāskara I is the approximation of sine function.

Trigonometry:

The sine function[38] which was proposed by Bhāskara I is:

$$\sin(\theta) = \frac{16\theta(180 - \theta)}{5(180)^2 - 4\theta(180 - \theta)},$$
$$given\ (0 \le \theta \le 180)$$

$$=> \sin(\theta) = \frac{4\theta(180 - \theta)}{40500 - \theta(180 - \theta)},$$

The above mentioned formula is present in the book Mahabhaskariya which was written by him.

The below mentioned sutra is quoted from the book Mahabhaskariya which is describing the above formula for sine function.

मख्यादि रहितं कर्म वक्ष्यते तत्समासतः ।
चक्राधार्शिक समूहाद्विशोध्या ये भुजांशका ॥ १७ ॥
तत्छेष गुणिता द्विष्ठाः शोध्याः खाभ्रेषुखाब्धितः ।
चतुर्थांशेन शेषस्य द्विष्ठमन्त्य फलं हतम् ॥ १८ ॥
बाहु कोट्योः फलं कृत्सनं क्रमोत्क्रम गुणस्य वा ।
लभ्यते चन्द्रतीक्ष्णांइवोस्ताराणां वापि तत्त्वतः ॥ १९ ॥

– Mahabhaskariya[39] VII, 17-19

His other significant contributions in Mathematics are:

1. Works in number zero.
2. Numbers in positional system.
3. Prime numbers.

Chapter 7

Kātyāyana

Introduction

Kātyāyana[40] was born on around 6th to 3rd century BCE in a Brahmin family and acquired knowledge from Vedas. He was a great mathematician, author, Vedic priest and a grammarian.

Theories

The main work of Kātyāyana on mathematics was Sulbasutras. We have studied about Sulbasutras in the previous chapter of Baudhāyana. The Sulbasutras which was composed by Kātyāyana was named as Kātyāyana Sulbasutras. Sulbasutras is a book of geometry.

There was another book which was on grammar named Vārttikakāra[41].

There are four are important Sulbasutras and those are: Baudhāyana (It is available in chapter 2), Āpastamba, Mānava and Kātyāyana.

There are 6 chapters in Kātyāyana Śulbasūtras[42,43] and 67 sutras in those 6 chapters. Kātyāyana Sulbasutras deals with the east-west lines also known as *Prāci* (प्राची) which is necessary for construction of altars.

Chapter 8

Apastamba

Introduction

Apastamba[44] was a sage who lived approximately on around 600 BC according to some historians. He was one among the greatest mathematicians who wrote one of the texts of Śulbasūtras. In previous chapters we have read that Baudhāyana as well as Kātyāyana also had their own Śulbasūtras.

His main work in Śulbasūtras was the estimation of root 2. He used his mathematical skills to construct altars.

Fig 1.8.1: Apastamba[45]

Theories

Now let's talk about the mathematical contribution of Apastamba. His main contribution is the text of Śulbasūtras. The Śulbasūtras consist of construction of fire altars.

Śulbasūtras[46] by Apastamba consist of more than six chapters whereas Baudhāyana had only three. He estimated the value of $\sqrt{2}$ using the following formula:

$$\sqrt{2} = 1 + \frac{1}{3} + \frac{1}{3*4} - \frac{1}{3*4*34}$$

$$= 1.41421568611$$

From the above formula we can conclude that he estimated the value of $\sqrt{2}$ which is accurate up to 5 decimal places.

Chapter 9

Manava

Introduction

Manava[47], a mathematician, lived on around 750 BC, Vedic priest and author of Śulbasūtras. According to his writings although he was a priest still he had the skills of craftman, as it is mentioned above that he had written Śulbasūtras, but the oldest one was written by Baudhāyana.

Theories

Now we'll discuss about the content which was included by Manava in Śulbasūtras. Manava Śulbasūtras contain one text which describes how to construct a circle from rectangle as well as a square from circle in an approximate manner. There were a lot of different values of pi (π) in Śulbasūtras.

According to Manava the equation[48] for finding the value of pi (π) is as follows:

$$\pi = \frac{25}{8}$$

$$= 3.125$$

From the above formula we can conclude that he found the value of pi (π) which is accurate up to 1 decimal place.

Chapter 10

Mahāvīra or Mahaviracharya

Introduction

Mahāvīra or Mahaviracharya[49], profound mathematician, was born on around 9th century AD in Karnataka. He had a lot of contribution in mathematics specially on algebra. He was the author of the book *Gaṇitasārasaṅgraha*. He worked on the book during the reign of Rashtrakuta dynasty, King Amoghavarsha. He was also a teacher. There were more than 1,130 versified rules[50] as well as examples in the book *Gaṇitasārasaṅ graha* which was divided into 9 chapters. Those chapters include terminology, basic operations, reductions of fractions and some miscellaneous problems which include linear or quadratic equations.

Theories

Combination(^nC_r):

Mahāvīra in the book *Gaṇitasārasaṅ graha*[51] mentioned the general formula for combination. In mathematics the formula for ^nC_r is as follows:

$$^nC_r = \frac{n(n-1)(n-2)\ldots(n-r+1)}{r(r-1)(r-2)\ldots 1}$$

Fractions:

Mahāvīra has also mentioned about the addition of fractions[52] in his book *Gaṇitasārasaṅ graha*. This consist of method for finding addition of fractions of unequal denominators by finding L.C.M (Least Common Multiple) or niruddha.

Geometry:

The book *Gaṇitasārasaṅ graha* also contains the rule for finding area as well as circumference of elongated circle which is similar to ellipse[53] called *Ayatavritta*.

Formula given by him to find area of ellipse:

$$A = \sqrt{\pi \times a^2 \times \pi \times b^2}$$

$$A = \pi a b$$
$$A \ is \ area$$
$$a \ is \ major \ axis$$
$$b \ is \ minor \ axis$$

According to him, the formula of circumference which is not accurate but approximately correct is as follows:

$$C = 2\sqrt{6b^2 + 4a^2}$$

C is circumference, a is major axis, b is minor axis

Section II

Science, Astronomy and Yoga

Chapter 11

Aryabhatta

Introduction

In one of the earlier chapters of the previous section, we have read about Aryabhatta where we have discussed about his contribution to Mathematics.

In this chapter we will study his contribution to science. At the age of 23, he composed a book named Āryabhaṭīya. There were several discoveries related to Kinematics, Eclipse, rotation of earth, circumference of earth etc.

Fig 2.11.1: Aryabhatta
(https://upload.wikimedia.org/wikipedia/commons/a/af/2064_aryabhata-crp.jpg)

Physics

Kinematics

Aryabhatta in his book Āryabhaṭīya[54,55] stated that when two planets move in the opposite direction then time to meet both the planets is the distance amongst them divided by the sum of their velocities, or when two planets move in the same direction then the time to meet both the planets is the distance between them divided by the difference between their velocities.

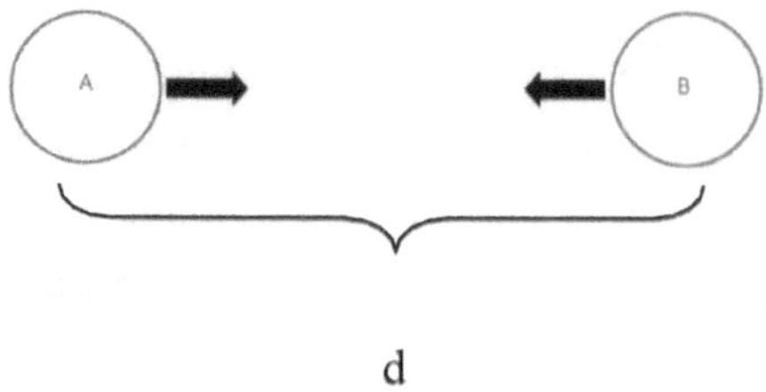

Mathematically:

Let velocity of A be 'v_1'

Let velocity of B be 'v_2'

Time to meet of **A** and **B** $= \dfrac{d}{v}$

where d is the distance between A and B and $v = v_1 + v_2$

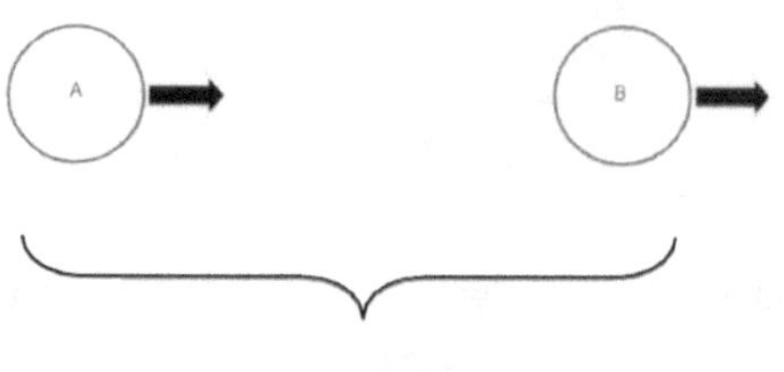

Let velocity of A be 'v₁'

Let velocity of B be 'v₂'

Time to meet $\mathbf{A}$ and $\mathbf{B} = \dfrac{\mathbf{d}}{\mathbf{V}}$

Where d is the distance between A and B and v = v_1-v_2 and v_1>v_2

Astronomy

Eclipse

Aryabhatta in his book Āryabhaṭīya mentioned about eclipse[56,57,58]. He described the eclipse as: The sun contains fire and the moon contains water and the sun gets obstructed by the moon and the moon gets obstructed by the shadow of the earth which causes eclipses.

Sidereal periods

Aryabhatta also calculated the sidereal rotation[59] of the earth. He calculated the period is 23 hours 56 minutes and 4.1 seconds. The modern figure is 23 hours 56 minutes and 4.091 seconds.

Other Discoveries

Some other discoveries[60,61] of Aryabhatta include:

1. Circumference of the earth
2. Motions of the solar system

Chapter 12

Varāhamihira

Introduction

In the chapter 4 of section 1 we have already studied about Varāhamihira and his contribution to mathematics where he described about his discoveries in the sector trigonometry, combination etc. Although he was a great mathematician but he was a scientist as well. His contribution in physics was remarkable. He had given several opinions on optics.

Fig 2.12.1: Varāhamihira
(https://qph.cf2.quoracdn.net/main-qimg-
400bb7779a00dca74d67a702468bdd48-lq)

Physics

Optics

As we have discussed above Varāhamihira was a great mathematician as well as a great physicist, his statement in physics is in the part of optics[62]. He had outlined the idea of reflection and refraction.

He stated that back-scattering of particles causes reflection. He also stated on refraction that when a ray of light travels from one medium to another medium, it bends. The cause of refraction is by the particle's ability of penetrating the inner spaces of material such as fluids.

Astronomy

Lustre of moon

The book *Panchsiddhantika*[63] which explains five earlier astronomical texts named *Surya Siddhanta, Romaka Siddhanta, Paulisa Siddhanta, Vasishtha Siddhanta* and *Pitamaha Siddhanta* written by Varāhamihira, is a revolutionary work in astronomy. He stated that due to sunlight the moon and other planets become lustrous.

Diameter of planets

Varāhamihira calculated the diameter of planets[64] of the solar system.

Other

Apart from optics Varāhamihira also contributed to Hydrology, Ecology as well as Geology. He is said to be one of those first scientists who claimed that plants and termites could indicate the presence of underground water.

He also gave a list of thirty plants as well as six animals which had the ability to indicate the presence of water.

Varāhamihira in *Brhat Samhita* proposed the earthquake cloud theory. The indication of earthquakes is enlightened in the thirty second chapter of *Brhat Samhita*[65].

Chapter 13

Kaṇāda

Introduction

Acharya Kaṇāda[66,67] whose original name was Aulukya or Ulūka lived sometime in between 6th to 2nd century BC, was a great scientist as well as a great philosopher. He had keen interest in minute particles also called *kana*, from there he got the name Kaṇāda. He had contributions in atomic theory. He also established Vaisheshika school of Indian philosophy. Apart from atomic theory, he also gifted laws of motion and gravitational laws as well.

Fig 2.13.1: Acharya Kaṇāda
(https://en.wikipedia.org/wiki/Ka%E1%B9%87%C4%81da_
%28philosopher%29#/media/File:Kanada.png)

Physics

Laws of motion

Acharya Kaṇāda proposed four laws of motion[68,69,70] which are similar to Newton's laws of motion.

The laws of motions are:

संयोगविभागवेगानां कर्म समानम् ॥ १ । १ । २० ॥

– Vaiseshika sutras 1.1.20

The above *sutra* means: *Karma* (Force) which is a common cause when two bodies collide or move away.

न द्रव्याणां कर्म ॥ १ । १ । २१ ॥

– Vaiseshika sutras 1.1.21

The above *sutra* means: The "*karma*" or the force has to be external and cannot be internal.

If we connect both the sentences then it becomes Newton's first law of motion which states that: "If a body is in the state of rest or uniform linear motion then it will remain in its own state unless compelled by an external unbalanced force".

Another law of Acharya Kaṇāda states that:

प्रयत्नविशेषान्नोदनविशेषः ॥ ५ । १ । ९ ॥

– Vaiseshika sutras 5.1.9

Meaning of the above statement is: Specific impulse is the outcome of specific effort. The above law resembles

Newton's second law of motion, which states that: "The rate of change of motion of a body is directly proportional to the force applied."

Another law:

$$कार्य्यविरोधि\ कर्म्म\ ||\ १\ |\ १\ |\ १४\ ||$$

– Vaiseshika sutras 1.1.14

The above law means: The action ("*karma*") is always opposed by the effect ("*karya*"). Newton's third law states that: "To every action there is an equal and opposite reaction".

Atomic Structure

We all know that atomic structure was given by several scientists like Sir John Dalton, Sir J.J. Thomson, Sir Ernest Rutherford and Sir Niels Bohr. We all praise them for their atomic structure, but very less amount of people know that Acharya Kaṇāda had given his own atomic structure on around 6th century BC.

According to Acharya Kaṇāda there are six *padarthas* in the universe and those are:

1. *Dravya* (Substance)
2. *Guna* (Attributes)
3. *Karma* (Action)
4. *Samanya* (Generality)
5. *Visesha* (Specificity)
6. *Samavaya* (Inherence)

From the above *padarthas*[71] there are 9 *Dravya*, 17 *Guna* and 5 *Karma*

पृथिव्यापस्तेजो वायुराकाशं कालो दिगात्मा मन इति द्रव्याणि ॥ १ । १ । ५ ॥

– Vaiseshika sutras 1.1.5

Meaning of the above statement is that there are 9 *Dravya* and those are:

1. *Pruthvi* (Earth)
2. *Apas* (Water)
3. *Tejas* (Fire)
4. *Vayu* (Air)
5. *Aakasha* (Space)
6. *Kaala* (Time)
7. *Dikh* (Direction)
8. *Atma* (Self)
9. *Manas* (Mind)

According to Acharya Kaṇāda the definition of atom is:

सदकारणवन्नित्यम् ॥ ४ । १ । १ ॥

तस्य कार्यं लिङ्गम् ॥ ४ । १ । २ ॥

– Vaiseshika sutras 4.1.1 and 4.1.2

The above two statements mean:

In nature everything that exists is eternal as well as uncaused, the proof is atom.

According to him properties[72,73] of atom is as follows:

1. One can subdivide everything.
2. The matter is made up of very small particles called *paramanu* (Atom).
3. *Paramanu* (atom) cannot further be divided
4. *Paramanu* (atom) is indestructible
5. Atoms are so minute that it is not observable to naked eye
6. Atoms of same substance combine to form *dvyanuka* (biatomic molecules) and *tryanuka* (triatomic molecules).
7. Through some processes like heat or other factors the atoms can combine in various ways to cause chemical changes.
8. There are two states of atoms and those are: state of absolute rest and motion.

Other Discoveries

Apart from the laws of motion and atoms he also stated several facts about:

1. Grutva which means gravity.
2. Laws of gravity.

Chapter 14

Brahmagupta

Introduction

In one of the previous chapters, we have studied about Brahmagupta and his contributions on Mathematics. Apart from Mathematics, he also contributed to Physics. He has given some theories on gravity as well as the structure of the earth and positions of different planets. In this chapter we are going to study about the contribution of Brahmagupta on science specially on Physics.

Fig 2.14.1: Brahmagupta
(https://d138zd1ktt9iqe.cloudfront.net/media/seo_landing_files/
image-001-1600757408.png)

Physics

Gravitation

Brahmagupta had a significant contribution on gravitational force.[74,75] He described that there is an attractive force known as *gurutvākarṣaṇ* which means gravity. He described it in the following way:

As nature of the earth to attract bodies towards itself so bodies fall towards the earth.

From the above statement it is clear that the attractive property of gravitation was mentioned by Brahmagupta. Before him Acharya Kaṇāda also stated about gravity.

Astronomy

Distance between the earth and the moon[76]

Brahmagupta calculated and stated that the distance between the earth and the moon is lesser than the distance between the earth and the sun.

Circumference of the earth

Brahmagupta proved that the earth is spherical in shape and he also calculated the circumference of the earth. According to him the circumference of the earth is 36,000 km which means 22,500 miles.

Others

Some of the other discoveries[77,78] that were done on science was calculating the solar year. After calculating the solar year, he found that there are 365 days 6 hours 5 minutes and 19 seconds in one year that is fairly accurate according to today's calculation which is 365 days 5 hours 48 minutes, and about 45 seconds.

Chapter 15

Nagarjuna

Introduction

In the previous three chapters of this section, we have discussed about the scientists those who dealt with Physics and Astronomy. Now let's go for the chapter where the contribution in field of Chemistry is introduced. In this chapter we are going to study the contributions of Nagarjuna, one of the greatest scientists of ancient India. His main work was related to Chemistry specially on Metallurgy and Alchemy.

Fig 2.15.1: Nagarjuna
(https://qph.cf2.quoracdn.net/main-qimg-b71eeb025053a9289baf10f
c9ff7fad2-lq)

Chemistry/Medicine

From the above introduction it is clear that Nagarjuna was a chemist whose main work dwells around metallurgy and alchemy. Now let us talk about his works. He had written a book named *Rasaratnakara*[79] which is based on alchemy. It is also considered to be one of the oldest documented texts in Sanskrit on Alchemy. Several alchemic and metallurgical experiments[80] were conducted by Nagarjuna. The objective of those experiments was to convert base elements to gold. It is believed that the gold-shine mechanism used by today's jewelry industry which is often referred as imitation which is a gift of Nagarjuna. In his book *Rasaratnakara* he mentioned about the methods for extracting[81] different metals like gold, silver, copper and tin. Some other contributions[82] of Nagarjuna are:

1. His book mentions about preparing mercury (*rasa*) compounds.
2. Extracting metals such as gold, silver etc. from their ores and purifying them.
3. Preparing medicinal drugs
4. He also wrote on metals as well as their stability.
5. He described how to prepare a medicine to increase lifespan.

Chapter 16

Sushruta

Introduction

Sushruta,[83,84] an ancient general physician as well as surgeon, lived sometime in between 1000 BC and 8th century BC. He is often considered as "Father of Surgery" and "Father of Plastics Surgery". He composed a book named *Sushruta Samhita* which is considered as one of the oldest texts in the field of plastic surgery and 'Great trilogy of Ayurvedic Medicine'[85] which includes *Astanga Hridaya* and *Charaka Samhita*. He also mentioned about several surgical instruments. We will discuss about his works in the upcoming topics.

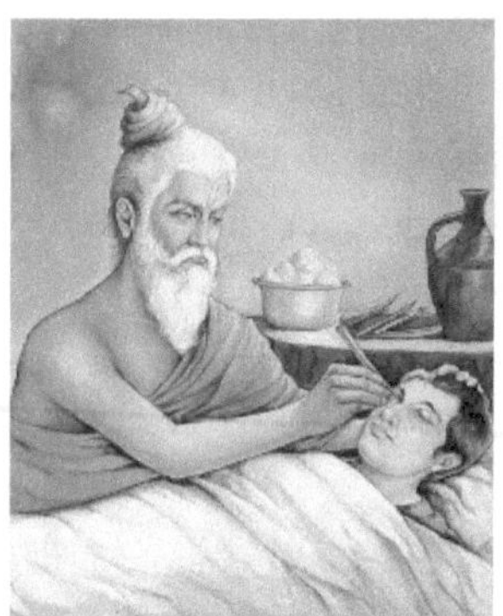

Fig 2.16.1: Sushruta
(https://qph.cf2.quoracdn.net/main-qimg-e3acf294357f4393ebcdca7c75
80bcd8.webp)

Medical Science

Rhinoplasty[86,87]

In skin grafts pieces of skin are transplanted from one portion of the body to another. Forehead flap Rhinoplasty is a type of surgery which is still active today where a thick piece of skin is taken from forehead and is used to reconstruct a nose. Now a days surgeon uses Skin grafts technique in order to restore areas where protective layers of tissues are lost due to infection, trauma, burns etc. These techniques are mentioned in the book *Sushruta Samhita*.

Cataract[88,89]

Now a days cataract operation is very common. This surgery is not new but very old as it was performed by Maharshi Sushruta. He was also a person to give an accurate and detailed description of varieties of cataract as well as about its surgery in his books *Sushruta Samhita*.

Tools[90,91]

Now let us talk about the tools which were used by Maharshi Sushruta for his surgery. He mentioned more than 100 instruments for surgery.

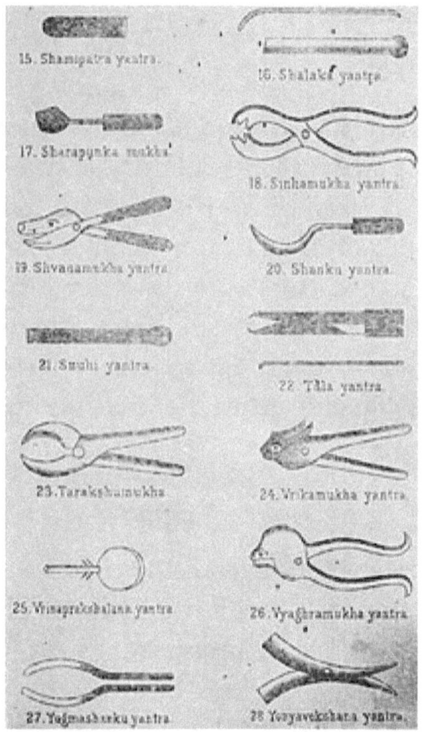

Fig 2.16.2: Surgical Instruments of Sushruta
(https://upload.wikimedia.org/wikipedia/commons/thumb/e/e0/Ancient_
Hindu_text_Sushruta_samhita_yantra%2C_surgical_instruments_4_
of_4.jpg/210px-Ancient_Hindu_text_Sushruta_samhita_yantra%2C_
surgical_instruments_4_of_4.jpg)

Others

Some other contributions[92,93,94] are:

1. Treatment of 12 types of fractures as well as 6 types of dislocation.
2. He also mentioned several ways of growing lost hair and removing the hairs.

Chapter 17

Charaka

Introduction

In the previous chapter we have learned about Sushruta and his contributions in the field of medical science. In this chapter we will study about Charaka[95] who is considered as the father of Ayurveda because of his enormous contributions in the same field. It is also considered that the book composed by him is *Charaka Samhita* which is the encyclopedia of Ayurveda. In the upcoming topics we will discuss about some of his contributions in Ayurveda.

Fig 2.17.1: Charaka
(https://www.hinduscriptures.com/wp-content/uploads/2019/06/charaka-233x300.jpg)

Medical Science

Metabolism/Immunity[96,97]

Charaka was a physician who presented the concept of metabolism as well as immunity. According to him a body functions as it contains three principles named as:

1. *Vata* which means movement.
2. *Pitta* that means transformations
3. *Kapha* which means stability

The above principles are produced while the *dhatus* which means the blood, marrows and flesh are acting upon the foods. Same quantity of food eaten by different body produces different amount of those principles. He further stated that illness is caused by the disturbed balance among the three principles.

Genetics[98,99]

Charaka described genetics and distributed it into three units and those are:

1. *Beej* (later on it was termed as Germinal cell)
2. *Beejbhag* (later on it was termed as Chromosome)
3. *Beejbhagavyava* (later on it was termed as Gene)

He also stated that genetic disorder in a child is due to the ovum or sperm of the parents, which is still accepted today.

Chapter 18

Patanjali

Introduction

Maharishi Patanjali[100,101] is often referred as father of modern Yoga. He was a spiritual leader. It is not well known about his birth but it is believed that he lived in between 2nd century BCE and 5th century CE. The term Yoga is derived from a Sanskrit word *Yoktra* which literally means connecting the mind towards inner-self and liberating beyond the outer senses. Maharishi Patanjali's contribution in the field of Yoga and medicine was incredible. He composed a book on Yoga named *Yoga Sutras*.

Fig 2.18.1: Maharishi Patanjali
(https://static.theprint.in/wp-content/uploads/2020/02/Maharishi-Patanjali-statue.jpg?compress=true&quality=80&w=376&dpr=2.6)

Yoga

Yoga Sutras[102]

Maharishi Patanjali who was also known as Gonardiya or Gonikaputra was the author of Yoga Sutras. It was documented sometime in between 500 BCE and 400 CE. Now let's see what is present in *Yoga Sutras*. In this script the yogic thoughts were categorized in four volumes and those four volumes are:

1. *Samadhi Pada*
2. *Sadhana Pada*
3. *Vibhuti Pada*
4. *Kaivalya Pada*

This book was divided into four chapters as we have discussed above which contains 196 aphorisms which means sutras and in which *Sadhana Pada* can be further divided into two systems of yoga and those are Kriya Yoga and Ashtanga Yoga.

Section III

Literature

Chapter 19

Kālidāsa

Introduction

Kālidāsa[103] was one of the greatest ancient Sanskrit poets and playwrights. He wrote poems and plays which are based on *Rāmāyana*, *Mahābhārata*, *Vedas* and *Purāṇas*. Some of his plays are: *Abhijñānaśākuntalam*, *Mālavikāgnimitram* etc. He wrote two epic poems which include *Kumārasambhavam* and Raghuvaṃśa and one minor poem which include *Meghadūta*.

Fig 3.19.1: Kālidāsa

(http://www.history-india.in/wp-content/uploads/2018/09/1-7.jpg)

Literature

Abhijñānaśākuntalam[104,105]

The play *Abhijñānaśākuntalam* is divided into seven acts. This play is considered as the last play by *Kālidāsa*. This play is inspired from a portion of the epic *Mahābhārata*. It is a love story of Sakuntala and King Dushyant.

Now let us go through a brief overview of the play:

Sakuntala was daughter of Rishi Vishwamitra and Menaka but both could not take her with them due to their personal reason, so the birds protected her until a sage named Kanava adopted her as her own child.

After few years Sakuntala grew up. One day Kanava was not in his cottage and King Dushyant met Sakuntala and they both fell in love with each other. They got wed-locked with each other (*gandharva* marriage) and the king gave his ring to Sakuntala as a token of love and promised that he would return and take Sakuntala to his kingdom.

One day sage Durvasa visited sage Kanava's cottage where only Sakuntala was present and she was deeply engrossed in the thought of king Dushyant, so she missed the sage's voice and failed to reply. Since no one responded, sage Durvasa cursed Sakuntala that about whom she was thinking, would forget her. After many requests from Sakuntala and her friends he altered the curse as he could not take it back that if she shows some object which belongs to the person, he would recognize her. One day sage Kanava arranges a visit of Sakuntala to the court of King Dushyant, on her way she stopped and drank water but unfortunately, she lost the ring which was presented by the king. The king fails to recognize Sakuntala who was pregnant because of the curse and Sakuntala was unable to show the ring as she lost it. So, Sakuntala went back to her cottage. Later the king got his ring back by a fisherman who found it in the belly of a fish. Therefore, Dushyant recognized her and felt guilty. He started searching her in every possible place. One day while searching, he found a child whose name was Bharat, playing with a cub. Then he came to know that the name of the child's mother was Sakuntala. Dushyant finally found her and asked her to forgive him and they returned to the kingdom.

Raghuvaṃśa[106,107]

Raghuvaṃśa is an epic poem written by Kālidāsa. There are nineteen *sargas* in this poem. This poem is based on the history of Ragu dynasty which means Dilipa and his successors up to Agnivarna. It is said to be one of the masterpieces of Kālidāsa. This poem deals with the great warrior Ragu who was ancestor of Lord Rama.

Others

Some other works are:

1. *Mālavikāgnimitram*
2. *Kumārasaṃbhavam*
3. *Meghadūta*
4. *Vikramōrvaśīya*

Chapter 20

Shudraka

Introduction

In the previous chapter we have studied about the contributions of Kālidāsa. In the current chapter we are going to study about another famous playwright whose name is Shudraka[108]. According to the prologue of the play *Mrichchhakatika*, he was a king. He performed *Ashvamedha* in order to prove his supremacy. He composed three plays in Sanskrit named: *Mrichchhakatika, Padmaprabhritaka* and *Vinavasavadatta*.

Literature

Mrichchhakatika[109,110,111,112]

Shudraka composed a Sanskrit play, *Mrichhakatika*. This is also popular by the name "The Little Clay Cart". The play revolves around Charudatta and Vasantasena, and their struggle for maintaining their relationship.

This play is a love story of a poor and noble Brahmin named Charudatta and a beautiful courtesan, Vasantasena. Samsthānaka, the king's brother-in-law who loved Vasantasena too, was a threat for the two lovers. Once Samsthānaka proposed love to Vasantasena but she rejected. So, he wanted to get her love by force.

He chased Vasantasena one day but fortunately she managed to save herself by hiding in Charudatta's house. She lied him that Samsthānaka chased her for the gold ornaments so she kept the ornaments in his house. Sarvilaka who was the lover of Madanika, servant of Vasantasena stole those ornaments from Charudatta's house in order to release her from duty. Upon seeing the ornaments Madanika suggested Sarvilaka to return those ornaments as a messenger of Charudatta. Vasantasena, upon hearing their conversation, released Madanika with Sarvilaka. Then Sarvilaka kept Madanika in a merchant's house as he went to rescue his friend Aryaka who was captured by the king.

Once Samsthānaka got a chance to kill Vasantasena, but by God's grace she was saved by a mendicant. After that Samsthānaka filed a case against Charudatta, who was sentenced to death for the murder of Vasantasena. Before beheading him Vasantasena revealed the truth and saved Charudatta.

Vina-Vasavadatta[113,114,115]

In the title of the play the *Vina* refers to a musical instrument and Vasavadatta is the heroine of the play. First eight acts of the play are available. Those manuscripts were discovered and kept in Kerala, but the last portion is lost. The first eight acts conclude that:

Father of Vasavadatta was king of Avanti named Pradyota who selects the king of Vatsa named Udayana as husband of Vasavadatta but because of his (Udayana's) pride he would have rejected her. To break his pride Pradyota arranged to capture Udayana in Ujjayini, the capital of Avanti, where he met Vasavadatta and fell in love with her. He used to meet her on the pretext of teaching her Vina. Rest of the play is unavailable.

Others

There is another play which was written by Shudraka named *Padmaprabhri- taka*.

Chapter 21

Vishakhadatta

Introduction

Vishakhadatta[116,117] was a Sanskrit poet and playwright. Very little is known about him. He presented the names of his father and grandfather as Maharaja Bhaskaradatta and Maharaja Vateshvaradatta in his political play *Mudrārākṣasa*. *Devichandraguptam* and *Mudrārākṣasa* are the only two known plays which were written by him. His period is not clear, some scholars believe that he stayed in or around 6th century CE and other believes that he lived on around late 4th century to early 5th century.

Literature

Mudrārākṣasa[118,119]

The main plot of the Sanskrit political thriller *Mudrārākṣasa* is how Chanakya, who served as the prime minister of the Mauryan emperor Chandragupta, directed Chandragupta by overthrowing the Nanda Empire and establishing the Mauryan dynasty. This play deals with the several themes such as power, betrayal, loyalty etc.

In this play Chanakya who was thrown out from the court of Dhana Nanda. So, Chanakya was determined to avenge and overthrow the Nanda dynasty. He met Chandragupta, whose objective was also to overthrow the Nandas. So, they both formed an alliance.

Chanakya allied with the Parvata from northwest. The above alliance assured Chandragupta triumph over Nanda. Both Chandragupta as well as Parvata divided the previous possessions of Nanda. Then Parvata was poisoned and murdered so his son named Malayaketu was enthroned as king. After that Malayaketu allied with a minister in the court of Dhana Nanda named Rakshasa. Then Malayaketu demanded all the old territories that belonged to Nanda. Then Malayaketu planned with his allies in order to attack Pataliputra which was the capital of Chandragupta. After that Chanakya managed to bring Rakshasa at the side of Mauryan king, Chandragupta and that resulted in breaking of the alliance between Rakshasa and Malayaketu.

Devichandraguptam[120]

Devichandraguptam also known as *Devichandragupta* is another play which was written by Vishakhadatta.

This play deals with king Ramagupta, his wife Dhruvadevi and his cousin Chandragupta. In this play Ramagupta was tricked into signing a humiliating written agreement with a Saka ruler.

Chandragupta the younger brother of king Ramagupta played the role of protagonist who took revenge by defeating and killing Saka ruler. Rest of the play is not clear but according to some scholars Chandragupta dethroned Ramagupta and was crowned as king of Gupta empire and he also married Dhruvadevi.

Chapter 22

Bhavabhūti

Introduction

Bhavabhūti[121,122], one of the greatest Sanskrit poets and playwrights was born in Padmapura, Vidarbha. It is considered that his plays are equal as the works done by Kālidāsa about whom we have already read in one of the previous chapters of this section. His original name was Srikantha Nilakantha. Some of his works are *Mahaviracharita*, *Malatimadhava* and *Uttararamacarita*.

Literature

Mahaviracharita[123,124]

The play *Mahaviracharita* which was composed by Bhavabhūti contains seven acts. Modern scholars believe that Bhavabhūti wrote the play up to 46th verse of Act V. There are two theories. First theory says that the rest of the play is lost and second theory says that he left the play unfinished.

This play is inspired from the early life of Lord Rama. The summary of the play is as follows:

The first act starts when Lord Rama with his brother Lakshmana and a sage Vishwamitra went to kill a demoness Tataka where they met Kushadhvaja whose niece was Sita. There the messenger of king of Lanka Ravana, Sarvamaya demands Sita for Ravana. Suddenly demoness Tataka attacked and Vishwamitra instructed Rama to kill the demoness and he did so. Kushadhvaja wished to have Lord Rama as his son in law. Then King Janaka imposed a condition that the one who would string the *Shiv Dhanush* would marry Sita. Tataka's sons Maricha and Subahu attacked and Subahu died and Maricha managed to escape.

Then the second act starts where Lord Parshurama warned Ravana to stop oppressing the sages of Dandaka Forest (*Dandakaranya*). Then Ravana's minister Malyavan provoked Parshurama against Rama as he broke the *Shiv Dhanush* and Lord Shiva was Parshurama's Guru. After that enraged Parshurama went to Mithila and met Rama who asked Parshurama to calm down.

Then in the third act the sage Vishwamitra, Vashishtha and Satananda tried to calm Parshurama but failed and Parshurama prepared for a battle.

Then in the fourth act Malyavan and Surpanakha (sister of Ravana) arrived at Mithila, there they came to know about Parshurama's defeat. Then Ravana planned to bring Lord Rama to the Dandaka Forest. In Dandaka Forest Ravana's demons and his friend Bali could get rid of Rama. Then Surpanakha in the guise of Manthara, a maid of Rama's step mother Kaikeyi, brought a letter which was false from Kaikeyi. The letter asked Dasharatha (Father of Rama and king of Ayodhya) to send Rama to the *vanavasa* for 14 years of exile followed by crowning Kaikeyi's son

Bharata as king. Rama with his wife Sita and brother Lakshmana left for the forest and started living in the mountain Chitrakuta.

In the fifth act at Panchavati, Lakshmana cut the nose of Surpanakha when she was lusting for Rama. The Vulture, Jatayu observed Rama and Lakshmana chasing a deer and, in the meantime, Ravana abducted Sita. Then Jatayu tried to save her and lost life. While dying Jatayu revealed the abduction of Sita to Rama. Then Lakshmana saved Shramana (one who joined Sugriva who was brother of Bali) by killing Kabandha. Then Malyavan provoked Bali to attack Rama. Bali confronted Rama and the act ends. Then the rest part of act V, VI and VII has two manuscripts like North Indian manuscript and South Indian manuscript.

Uttararamacarita[125,126]

This is a Sanskrit play based on the Uttara Khanda of the renowned epic the Ramayana which deals with the life of Lord Rama after he returned to Ayodhya. This play is divided into seven acts.

Now let us shed some light in the play:

In the beginning of the first act Sutradhar briefed introduction of *Ma* Sita and Lord Rama. Then it has been told that the citizens criticized Lord Rama for accepting Sita. They had a doubt in Sita's chastity, which forced helpless Rama to take a harsh decision to send Sita away. Lord Rama never questioned her chastity but he took such decision to satisfy the citizen though Rama never stopped thinking about Sita. Then Sita gave birth to Lava and Kusha. They grew under

Valmiki's guidance. The story then follows in a conclusion with their reunion.

Other Plays:

One more play which was written by Bhavabhūti is *Malatimadhava*.

Chapter 23

Harisena

Introduction

Harisena[127,128,129] was a Sanskrit poet in the court of king Samudragupta. He composed *Prayag Prasasti* which is a description of the valor of the king Samudragupta on around 345 CE which is inscribed on the Allahabad Pillar. He encouraged the culture, art and Buddhist architecture. In accordance with a lawyer named Arthur Berriedale Keith *"Harisena's poem bears expressly the title Kavya, though it consists both of prose and verse. Its structure is similar to the delineation of kings adopted in the prose romances of Subandhu and Bana"*. He had a keen interest in playing lute.

Literature

Prayag Prashasti[130]

Prayag Prashasti was composed by the famous poet Harisena. The Sanskrit word *Prashasti* means to praise someone. During those periods poets used to praise their kings using *Prashasti*. From the above introduction we learned that Harisena was a poet in the Samudragupta's court so he praised king Samudragupta in his *Prashasti* which is inscribed on the Ashokan pillar in Allahabad which is now known as Prayagraj. It provides a detailed description about the king Samudragupta, like his greatness, his interests etc.

Let's observe what is engraved on Ashokan pillar and briefly describe what is written in it:

From the *Prashasti* which was composed by Harisena we come to know that:

Samudragupta was an outstanding warrior.

1. In order to expand his kingdom or empire he fought numerous battles.
2. King Samudragupta had a keen interest in arts, music and poems so he used to encourage all of them which were present in his court.
3. In the *Prashasti* he is described as God.

Chapter 24

Bhāsa

Introduction

Bhāsa[131,132] is considered as one of the oldest Sanskrit playwrights or a dramatist. Not much is known about his life. His most plays were lost but those were revived by an Indian scholar named Ganapati Shastri. There are many plays written by him among those his best work is *Svapnavasavadattam*. Most of his plays are based on the epics, *Ramayana* and *Mahabharata*. The plays are based on *Ramayana* like *Yagna-Phalam, Pratima-nataka, Abhisheka-natka* and some of his plays are based on *Mahabharata* like *Panch-ratra, Duta-Ghattotkacha, Madhyama-vyaYoga, Harivamsa* or *Bala-charita* etc. His plays are not so long like later playwrights.

Literature

Svapnavasavadattam[133,134]

The play *Svapnavasavadattam* which was composed by the poet Bhāsa is a sequel to one of his plays named *Pratijnayaugandharayana* which deals with how the king Udayana was trapped by the king Pradyota and king Pradyota's daughter Vasavadatta used to take music lesson from the trapped king and they fell in love with each other and eloped by the help of his minister Yaugandharayana.

Now let us talk about the play *Svapnavasavadattam*. The play *Svapnavasavadattam* was lost which was recovered by an Indian Scholar named T. Ganapati Shastri.

A brief overview of the play is as follows:

The king Udayana had lost all his territories which was under the king Aruni. The minister of king Udayana named Yaugandharayana wanted to recover all the lost territories, so a friendly relationship between the king Udayana and the king of Magadh is necessary. To increase the friendly relationship the king Udayana must marry Padmavati who was the sister of the king of Magadh. Udayana was vehemently refusing to marry Padmavati because of his intense love for Vasavadatta, so Yaugandharayana planned and asked Vasavadatta to help him. Yaugandharayana spread a news when the king was in a hunting expedition that Vasavadatta and Yaugandharayana died in a fire which consumed the village of Lavanaka. Then Yaugandharayana and Vasavadatta left the place in disguise and reached a hermitage where they met princess Padmavati. Yogadharayana, disguised as a recluse, gives Vasavadatta the charge of Padmavati, and claimed that she is his sister and her husband has gone on a journey. Then Vasavadatta adapted the name Avantika and starts living with the princess Padmavati. Then the king agreed to marry Padmavati, but his love for Vasavadatta was still strong. One day Padmavati gets a headache, so an Ocean Pavilion was arranged for her to sleep. The king went there but could not found Padmavati and falls fast asleep, meanwhile Vasavadatta reached there in order to comfort Padmavati and sat on the bed but on realising that the person sleeping was king who was addressing Vasavadatta in his dream, she moved away from there. After waking up the king got a pleasant news that the king Aruni was defeated and his territories were recovered. One day a messenger arrives from Ujjain to congratulate Udayana for his victory and presents a picture which contains Vasavadatta. Then Padmavati recognized Vasavadatta in the picture then Yaugandharayana arrived and disclosed the secret.

Karnabharam[135,136,137]

This play describes about the tension of Karna on the previous day of the War of Kurukshetra. There are several deviations from the original epic. This play is a part of the famous epic the Mahabharata.

Now let us read a brief overview of the play:

After the death of Dronacharya, the generalship of the army of Kaurava was transferred to Angraj Karna. Duryodhan informs Karna that the battle is about to begin. After getting ready for the war suddenly the promise which was given by him to his mother Kunti came to his mind. Then he describes how he learned to use weapons from his teacher Parashurama disguised as a *brahmin*. One day Parashurama slept on the lap of Karna, a worm ripped his thigh but he did not move so that his *Guru* did not wake up. But as soon as the blood which was oozed out from his thighs touched Parashurama, he woke up and learned the truth and in anger he cursed him that all his (Karna's) weapons would fail in his need.

When Karna asked Salya, king of *Madra*, to lead his chariot towards Arjuna in the battle field, he was stopped by a *brahmin* and asked for a boon from Karna and on asking what he wanted, he asked for the armor of Karna. Karna satisfied the *brahmin* who was Indra in disguise. After receiving the armor Indra departed but since he was full of remorse, Indra gifted him Vimala Astra through an angel as a return gift which was then accepted by Karna. At the end of the play Karna asked Salya to move towards the battle field.

Other plays

There are several other plays which were written by him. Name of some of the plays written by him are:

Pratijnayaugandharayana: It is a play of four acts and it is the prequel of another play written by him and which is *Svapnavasavadattam*.

Plays which are based on the epic *Mahabharata*:

1. *Panch-ratra*
2. *Madhyama-vyaYoga*
3. *Duta-Ghattotkacha*
4. *Harivamsa or Bala-charita*
5. *Urubhanga*
6. *Duta-Vakya*

Plays which are based on the epic *Ramayana*:

1. *Pratima-nataka*
2. *Abhisheka-natka*
3. *Yagna-Phalam*

Chapter 25

Bāṇabhaṭṭa

Introduction

Bāṇabhaṭṭa[138,139] was a Sanskrit poet as well as prose writer of 7th century and was the Asthana Kavi in the royal court of king Harsha Vardhana. His main works include the biography of king Harsha Vardhana named *Harshacharita*. He also composed one of the world's oldest novels named *Kadambari*. Other works done by him were dramas named *Pārvatīpariṇaya* and *Caṇḍikāśataka*. A description about his early life and his ancestry can be recovered from the introduction of Kadambari. He was born to Rājadevi and Chitrabhānu in a Bhojaka family.

Literature

Kadambari[140,141,142]

Kadambari is a timeless classic novel in Sanskrit which was composed by Bāṇabhaṭṭa but unfortunately, he could not finish it as he perished which was later completed by his son named Bhushanabhatta. This is one of the earliest romantic novels in the world which is considered as a masterpiece of Indian literature.

The novel dwells around two love stories one between Kadambari and Chandrapeeda and another between Pundarika and Mahasveta. How Pundarika, an ascetic and

Mahasveta fell in love with each other. Then due to several reasons Pundarika died and Mahasveta started waiting for him as they would reunite. There was a friend of Pundarika named Kapinjala who was cursed due to several reasons and Pundarika then took a birth as the son of Sukanasa, the minister of the king of Ujjayini named Tarapida and since before dying Pundarika cursed the *Moon* due to some reason so the Moon was born as the son of Tarapida. The son of Sukanasa was named as Vaisampayana and the son of Tarapida was named as Chandrapeeda. As Kapinjala was cursed so he took birth as Chandrapeeda's horse with the name Indrayudha. One day Chandrapeeda met Mahasveta who narrated the whole story of her past and also told that her friend Kadambari was also suffering with her as she had taken an oath that until and unless Mahasveta was getting her love back, she would also not marry. Then Chandrapeeda met Kadambari and both fell in love with each other. One day Vaisampayana met Mahasveta and fell in love with her but she could not reciprocate the love as she loved Pundarika and cursed Vaisampayana for his repeated approach that he would become a parrot. Then Vaisampayana died and was born as a parrot and on hearing about Vaisampayana's death, Chandrapeeda also ended his life. Indrayudha also jumped into a lake and died, from there Kapinjala arose and told Mahasveta everything. Then Chandrapeeda was reborn as Sudraka the king of Vidisha. Then after many complications the parrot reached Sudraka's court and narrated the whole history. After listening to the story Sudraka died and Chandrapeeda emerged from there and married Kadambari. There the parrot also died and then Pundarika was revived and married Mahasveta.

Other works

Other than *Kadambari* his other works include:

1. *Pārvatīpariṇaya*
2. *Caṇḍikāśataka*
3. *Harshacharita*

Chapter 26

Bharavi

Introduction

Bharavi[143,144] was a Sanskrit poet who lived on around 6th century and was the writer of one of the six classical Sanskrit epics which are classified as *Mahakavya* and he was also the writer of the poem *Kirātārjunīya*. He is often considered as Kalidas's contemporary.

Kirātārjunīya, is considered as Bharavi's renowned work. His actual name was Damodara. He flourished during the reign of King Simhavishnu of Pallava dynasty and King Durvinita of Western Ganga dynasty.

Literature

Kirātārjunīya[145,146]

This epic poem narrates the battle between Arjuna, the third *Pandava* from *Mahābhārata*, and the *Kirāta* king (Lord Shiva), who was in the guise of a hunter. The poem began with Arjuna who was seeking for divine weapons and performing penance in the forest. During that time, he encountered and rejected the advances of Urvasi, a celestial nymph. As a result, she cursed him to become an eunuch for a year.

Arjuna then came across Lord Shiva, disguised as a hunter, and they engaged in a terrifying battle. In spite of Arjuna's prowess, he was eventually defeated by Lord Shiva, who then revealed his true identity. Arjuna then performed a ritual to worship him. The poem also portrayed the *Kirāta* people as skilled hunters who lived in harmony with nature.

Kirātārjunīya is renowned for its intricate wordplay and descriptions of nature. The poem highlights the importance of righteous conduct and the power of devotion to the Gods. It is regarded as one of the finest examples of Sanskrit poetry and continued to be studied and admired by many scholars and worldwide readers.

Section IV

Architecture

Note: It is very difficult to get the names of the architect of different historical architectures, so instead of the names of the architects, names of the kings or dynasty is mentioned.

Chapter 27

Ajanta Caves

Fig 4.1.1: Ajanta Caves
(https://upload.wikimedia.org/wikipedia/commons/c/c3/
Ajanta_%2863%29.jpg)

Overview

Ajanta Caves[147] are located in a city of Maharashtra named Sambhajinagar formerly known as Aurangabad. These were constructed in two phases in which the first phase began on around 2nd century BCE and there are two texts for second phase, according to the older text the construction of second phase of the caves was from 400 to 650 CE and according to later scholars the second phase was from 460 to 480 CE.

History

Satvahan Period[148,149]

In this section we will study about the construction of the caves which were done during Satvahan Period. During this period the caves 9, 10, 12, 13 and 15A were built and is considered as the earliest built caves. These caves are built according to the Hinayana sect of Buddhism. Among these caves, cave 9 and 10 contain Buddhist stupas which contains worship halls. The caves 12, 13 and 15A contains *viharas*.

Vākāṭaka Period [150-153]

According to historians, the construction of the second phase of Ajanta Caves began during the reign of a king of Vākāṭaka dynasty named Harisena. These caves are built according to Mahayana sect of Buddhism. The caves which were built during this period were 1 to 8, 11 and 14 to 29 among which 19, 26, and 29 are considered as *chaitya grihas* and rest are said to be *viharas*.

Architecture

Ajanta Caves[154,155] were constructed from the basalt and granite rock. The accumulation of rocks was due to the volcanic eruptions which took place long back. The workers not only carved the rocks in a planned way but also carved idols, roofs as well as pillars out of the rocks. There is a gateway between cave 15 and 16 which is decorated with snakes and elephants through which the tourists can enter.

Chapter 28

Sanchi Stupa

Fig 4.2.1: Sanchi
(https://cdn.britannica.com/36/155836-050-89E7AA9E/Great-Stupa-Sanchi-India.jpg)

Overview

Sanchi Stupa[156] is an Indian monument which is located at Madhya Pradesh and which was commissioned on around 3rd century BCE by the famous king of Maurya dynasty, Emperor Ashoka, and the expansions were done in different periods. The architecture is considered as of Buddhist style. This is also considered as one of the oldest Buddhist monuments.

History

Construction

When the great king Ashoka constructed[157,158] the great stupa, it had a massive hemispherical brick which covered the relics of the Lord Buddha in its center, with an elevated terrace around the base, an umbrella of stone and a balustrade was on the top in order to indicate the high rank. The present structure was constructed during Shunga period when the bricks were replaced by the stones and the diameter of the dome was doubled as well.

Architecture

The toranas and fencing have been made after the modeling of bamboo crafts of the surrounded areas. Initially bricks were used for the construction[159], afterwards it was covered with stone, Vedica and torana (gateway). The stupa consists of four entrances among which southern one was the first to get completed.

The height of the building is 54 feet and its width is of 120 feet. It has both upper as well as lower circumambulatory path. It has four toranas which depicts various incidents that has been taken from the life of Lord Buddha and Jatakas.

This monument has three fundamental features and those are:

1. Hemispherical mound
2. Square railing
3. Central pillar which is supporting a triple-umbrella

Some secondary features are:

1. Circular terrace which is also called *medhi*
2. Enclosed wall with entrance decorated in cardinal directions.

Chapter 29

Ellora Caves

Fig 4.3.1: Ellora Caves
(https://whc.unesco.org/uploads/thumbs/site_0243_0001-1200-630-201511041 52442.jpg)

Overview

Ellora[160] has a series of 34 magnificent rock-cut temples in the western part of India as well as in the northwest-central Maharashtra in Sambhaji Nagar (Aurangabad) district among which 12 Buddhist temples are in the south. There are 17 Hindu temples in the center and 5 Jain temples in the north. This is also designated as UNESCO World Heritage site on 1983[161].

History

Among those 34 rock-cut temples let us see the time period of their construction:

1. 12 Buddhist temples were constructed in between 200 BCE and 600 CE
2. 17 Hindu temples were constructed in between 500 to 900 CE
3. 5 Jain temples were constructed in between 800 to 1000 CE

Architecture

In the above sections we have discussed about the time period and the number of temples in the Ellora caves. Now let us talk about the architecture of the different types of caves.

The designs of the Hindu caves are most melodramatic. All the Buddhist caves consist of simple ornaments. There are some caves which consist of sleeping cell which is carved for itinerant monks.

Cave 13 to 29 consists of Hindu monuments like Kailāśa temple which is in cave 16, Rameshwar temple[162,163] which is in cave 21, Dhumar Lena[164] which is in cave 29, The Dashavatara which is in cave 15 etc.

Caves 1 to 12 consists of Buddhist monuments among which the Vishvakarma Cave[165] is notable which is cave 10.

Caves 30 to 34 consists of Jain monuments. These five Jain caves belong to Digambara sect. Chhota Kailasha is in cave 30 and the Indra Sabha is in cave 32 etc.

Chapter 30

Pattadakal Monuments

Fig 4.4.1: Pattadakal
(https://upload.wikimedia.org/wikipedia/commons/0/03/
Pattadakal_000.JPG)

Introduction

Pattadakal[166,167] is also known as Raktapura as well as Paṭṭadakallu. The literal meaning of the word Pattadakal is coronation place. This was complex of temples of both Hindus as well as Jains.

This complex is situated in Karnataka and lies on the west bank of the river Malaprabha. It is also awarded as UNESCO World Heritage Site. This complex consists of 9 Shiva temples and 1 Jain temple.

Architecture

We have discussed in the introduction part that there are 10 temples which include 9 Shiv temples and 1 Jain temple. The monuments of Pattadakal contain combinations of two major Indian styles of architecture which means both north Indian as well as south Indian. Four temples were built according to the North Indian Nagara style, four were built according to the Chalukya Dravida style and the last temple named as Papanatha temple which contains the touch of both the styles. Among all these, the oldest temple is Sangameshwara that was constructed in between 697 and 733 CE. Virupaksha Temple is considered as the largest temple in the Pattadakal that was constructed in between 740 and 745 CE. The Jain Narayana temple was built during the reign of Krishna II of Rashtrakutas on around 9th century.

Temples

Now let us see the description of all the temples.

Kadasiddheshwara temple[168,169]

According to Archaeological Survey of India this temple belonged to 7th century CE but as per George Michell this temple belonged to 8th century. This temple is facing east side and constructed around a square sacrum sanctum. It is holding a *linga* on a solid platform. The Nandi *Maharaj* (the bull) is facing it from outside. The spire is of northern Nagara style and a *sukanasa* (decorative feature on the entrance of *garbhagriha*) which includes Nataraja with Parvati projecting towards the east.

The external walls of the Kadasiddheshwara sanctum contains images of *Ardhanarishvara* that is half Lord Shiva and half Goddess Parvati which lies on its north. On its west, there lies *Harihara* that is half Lord Shiva and half Lord Vishnu. *Lakulisha* lies on its south.

Jambulingeshwara temple[170]

Another name of this east facing temple is Jambulinga temple. According to Archaeological Survey of India as well as Michell the construction of this temple was completed on around mid of 7th and early 8th century correspondingly. This is also constructed around a square sacrum sanctum whose external wall consists of *devakoshtha*. The frame canvases the images of Lord Vishnu on its north, Lord Surya on its west and *Lakulisha* to the south.

The temple is of northern rekha-nagara style, the kalasha and amalaka are of northern style but unfortunately, they got damaged. The entrance of the temple has been ornamented with three *shakhas* and each of them are with *purnakumbhas* under their capitals.

Galaganatha Temple[171]

This temple is situated to the east side of Jambulingeshwara temple. According to the estimation of Archaeological Survey of India this temple was built on around mid of 8th century but on contrary Michell estimated it to be in the late 7th century. This temple is also of northern rekha-nagara style and inside the sanctum of the temple there is a *linga* with a vestibule and on the outside of the temple there is Nandi *Maharaj* (the bull) facing the sanctum.

There are several mandapas in the temple for example community and social hall which is used to perform several ceremonial functions and there is also a *mukha mantapa*. The entrance of the pavilion is surrounded by the river Ganga and Yamuna.

The southern part of the temple contains a carved slab depicting eight armed Shiva who is killing Andhaka, the demon. The crypt of the eastern foundry contains the Panchatantra fables.

Chandrashekhara Temple[172,173]

This temple which has no tower, is facing east. It is located on southern side of Galaganatha temple. According to the Archaeological Survey of India this temple was constructed on around mid of 8th century whereas according to Michell the temple was built on around late 9th or early 10th century.

There is a *garbha griha* in this temple where a Shiva *linga* is installed and Nandi *Maharaj* (the bull) who is sitting in front of the *linga*. The sanctum of the Chandrashekhara temple contains a *devakostha* which means a niche in the wall on the either side. This temple contains *dvarapala* which means a guardian on each and every side of the entrance.

Sangameshwara Temple[174-180]

This temple also known as Vijayeshvara temple which is in Dravida style and is situated in the southern part of Chandrashekhara temple. According to several inscriptions in the temple and other evidences this temple was built on around 720 CE to 733 CE. Due to the death of king Vijayaditya on around 734 CE this temple was left unfinished, and it was completed in later centuries.

The temple is having a square layout whose sanctum is facing east and is surrounded by a covered circumambulatory path illuminated by three carved windows. Shiv *linga* is present inside the sanctum. The walls of the temple consist of many niches and images of Vishnu and Shiva which are carved in it. The themes like, *Shaivism, Vaishnavism* and *Shaktism* are carved in the temples among which *Shaivism* is represented by *Ardhanarishvara* (half Parvati and half Shiva), Nataraja etc., *Vaishnavism* is represented by avatars of Vishnu which include Varaha lifting goddess earth.

Kashivishweswara Temple[181,182]

Kashivishweswara Temple, located at Pattadakal, is either built between late 7th century to early 8th century or mid of 8th century. This temple also has a *garbha griha* where there is a *linga* and towards the east of the *garbha griha* there is a Nandi-mantapa contains the image of Nandi *Maharaj* (the bull). There is a *pranala* in the temple which is required to drain water out during any kind of devotional activities. The temple also contains an *antarala* which connects the mantapa with the entrance. The mouldings on which the temple is present contains the carvings of lions, peacocks, elephants etc.

The pillars and pilasters of the temples carved with several scripts of the *Ramayana*, the *Bhagavata Purana* and the *Shiva Purana*. There is one frieze which is portraying Ravana lifting the Kailasha as well as pranks of Krishna.

Mallikarjuna Temple[183-186]

According to some local inscriptions another name of Mallikarjuna Temple is Trailokeshwara Maha Saila Prasada. This temple is situated in the southern side of Kashivishweswara temple. This Shiva temple was sponsored by queen Trailokyamahadevi and was built on around mid of 8th century.

This temple also contains sanctum with Shiv *linga* and in the front of the sanctum there is an *antarala* with small temples of Goddess Durga as *Mahishasuramardini*. There is Nandi *Maharaj* (the bull), facing the sanctum. The temple is full of carved stones in order for storytelling. Pillars of the in the community hall of the temple canvas scriptures of *Puranas*. These stories include tradition of *Vaishnavism, Shaktism, Shaivism* as well as the *Rasa leela* of Shree Krishna from *Bhagavata Purana*.

Virupaksha Temple[187-198]

This temple is situated in the southern part of the Mallikarjuna temple. This temple is considered as the largest temple at Pattadakal. According to certain inscriptions this temple was built on around 740 CE and as it was sponsored by queen Lokmahadevi so it was also referred as "Shri Lokeshvara Mahasila Prasada". The chief architect of the temple whose name was Gunda Anivaritacharya was honored with *perijereppupatta* by king Vikramaditya-II.

The Virupaksha Temple is also facing east and also contains a square sanctum with a *linga*. There is one *antarala* which contains two shrines which is facing towards the images of lord Ganesha and goddess Parvati killing the buffalo demon.

The carvings in the sanctum walls represent images of deities of *Shaktism, Shaivism* as well as *Vaishnavism*. Deities such as Varaha, Narasimha, Harihara, Nataraja, Bhairava, Lakulisa, Brahma, Saraswati, Lakshmi, Durga etc.

There are several friezes such as two men wrestling with each other, rishi with Shiva, rishi with Vishnu, Gajendra elephant who was trapped in a lotus pond by a crocodile rescued by Vishnu etc. Some other carvings are Indra on an elephant and Surya with Aruna riding the chariot. Some scenes are from the epic *Ramayana* such as the golden deer, struggles of Rama and Lakshmana, Sita being kidnapped and many more. Several other friezes depict scenes from the epic *Mahabharata* such as birth of Shree Krishna after Vasudeva was imprisoned by Kamsa, story of Shree Krishna according to *Bhagavata Purana* as well as *Harivamsa* etc.

Papanatha Temple[199]

Papanatha temple, located in the south of Virupaksha temple, was built on around mid of 8th century. This temple is a mixture of Nagara and Dravida style. In the temples there are two *mantapas* both consists of 16 and 4 pillars. The pilastered niches and the tower are in the *Nagara* style whereas parapets and some other parts are in the *Dravida* style.

Just like the above temples this temple also east facing and linga is present in the sanctum. The only difference is that in this temple there is no Nandi- mandapa but there is an image of Nandi *Maharaj* (the bull) facing the sanctum.

The walls of the temple are carved with the themes and deities of both *Vaishnavism* as well as *Shaivism*. Some carved panels are depicting the epic *Ramayana* as well as some parts of *Kiratarjuniya*.

Jain Narayana Temple[200,201]

The Jain Narayana Temple was built on around 9th century. This temple was sponsored by the Kalyani Chalukyas or Krishna II who was the king of Rashtrakuta dynasty. This temple is different from the above temples as this temple consists of a carved Jina statue, situated at the northern side of *kapota* eave.

This temple also contains a square sanctum, an antechamber, a circumambulatory path, a porch and a *mantapa* which is divided into seven sections on the north and south walls. The walls contain niches where Jinas are seating. The sections are in the North Indian style. The entrance has the life-sized elephant torso carvings along with its riders.

References

[1-4]   Shah, Jayant. (2021). A HISTORY OF PIṄGALA'S COMBINATORICS. Northeastern University, Boston, Mass

[5]   https://www.cuemath.com/learn/pingala-mathematician/

[6-10]   Shah, Jayant. (2021). A HISTORY OF PIṄGALA'S COMBINATORICS. Northeastern University, Boston, Mass

[11],[13],[15],[16],[17]   https://www.cuemath.com/learn/baudhayana/

[12],[14]   T. A. Sarasvati Amma (1979), Geometry in ancient and medieval India, Motilal Banarsidass Publications, Delhi

[18]   Dr. Chetan Kumar Sahu (2021), ARYABHATT: A BEACON OF MATHEMATICS, International Journal of Multidisciplinary Education Research, VOLUME:10, ISSUE:10(2)

[19]   Namrata khadsang (2019), Value of pi (π), International Journal of Innovative Science and Research Technology, Volume 4, Issue 7, Maharashtra

[20-23]   Amulya Kumar Bag (1969), SINE TABLE IN ANCIENT INDIA

[24-26],[27],[29] Subrata, Bhowmik. (2010). GREAT INDIAN MATHEMATICIANS OF POST-CHRISTIAN ERA. Bulletin of Tripura Mathematical Society. XXX. 11-24.

[28] https://www.javatpoint.com/brahmagupta

[30-34] https://en.wikibooks.org/wiki/Timeless_Theorems_of_Mathematics/Brahmagupta_Theorem#cite_note-1

[35] https://en.wikipedia.org/wiki/Brahmagupta#cite_note-Plofker_Brahmagupta_quote_Chapter_12-22

[36] https://medium.com/montelle/brahmaguptas-interpolation-formula-f93be8e1410c

[37] https://www.cuemath.com/learn/bhaskara-i/

[38] R. C. Gupta (1967) "Bhāskara I's approximation to sine", Indian Journal of History of Science 2.2, pp. 121–36

[39] K. S. Shukla (1960) Mahabhaskariya, Lucknow University, pp. 45

[40-41] https://en.wikipedia.org/wiki/K%C4%81ty%C4%81yana

[42] https://ancientskiesbook.com/2021/05/katyayana-and-sulba-sutra.html

[43] Venkatesha Murthy, "Indian Mathematics", iACT, Bangalore

[44-46] Wilder, Brittany Kirby, Biography of a Mathematician: Apastamba, Math 200-102, October 30, 2013

[47] https://mathshistory.st-andrews.ac.uk/Biographies/ Manava/

[48] Gupta, R.C. (July 1988). "New Indian Values of π from the Mānava Súlba Sūtra". Centaurus. 31 (2): 114– 125

[49] https://indiansciences.in/mathematics-and-astronomy/mahavira-a-mathematical-prodigy-of-the-ancient-india

[50] https://tfipost.com/2021/01/mahaviracharya-mahavira-jain-the- great-9th-century-mathematician/

[51-53] https://indiansciences.in/mathematics-and-astronomy/mahavira-a-mathematical-prodigy-of-the-ancient-india

[54] WALTER EUGENE CLARK (1930), THE ĀRYABHAṬĪYA of ĀRYABHAṬA, THE UNIVERSITY OF CHICAGO PRESS, ILLINOIS

[55] https://www.youtube.com/watch?v=QzAub_ EjkZU&t=39s

[56] WALTER EUGENE CLARK (1930), THE ĀRYABHAṬĪYA of ĀRYABHAṬA, THE UNIVERSITY OF CHICAGO PRESS, ILLINOIS

[57] https://en.wikipedia.org/wiki/Aryabhata

[58] https://www.youtube.com/watch?v=jgjcy04PDRM& t=1447s

[59] R.C.Gupta (1997), "Āryabhaṭa", In Helaine Selin (ed.), Encyclopaedia of the history of science, technology, and medicine in non-western cultures

[60] https://www.livemint.com/Sundayapp/8wRiLexg 1N2IOXjeK2BKcL/How-Aryabhata-got-the-earths-circumference-right-millenia-a.html

[61] https://en.wikipedia.org/wiki/Aryabhata#cite_note-Selin1997-32

[62] https://www.mythoworld.com/varahamihira-the-multi-talented-genius-sage/

[63] https://www.mysteryofindia.com/2016/03/varahamihira-predicted-water-on-mars.html

[64] https://en.wikipedia.org/wiki/Surya_Siddhanta

[65] SCIENTISTS OF ANCIENT INDIA, Chapter 15, Indian Culture and Heritage, pp. 229-235, NIOS, updated on 10.09.2020

[66] SCIENTISTS OF ANCIENT INDIA, Chapter 15, Indian Culture and Heritage, pp. 229-235, NIOS, updated on 10.09.2020

[67] https://en.wikipedia.org/wiki/Ka%E1%B9%87%C4%81da_(philosopher)

[68] THE SACRED BOOKS OF THE HINDUS., EDITED BY MAJOR B. D, BASU, I.M.S-Retd., THE VIJAYA PRESS 1923

[69] https://www.youtube.com/watch?v=YB9c34 jAJKo&t=255s

[70] Priyank Bharati, Acharaya Kanada: Father of Physics and true inventor of law of motions, International

Journal of Science and Engineering, Volume-2 | Issue-10 | October,2016

[71]   THE ATOMIC THEORY in Ancient India || A film on Vaiseshika Sutras || Project SHIVOHAM, [https://www.youtube.com/watch?v=goMuN6CbZpU&t=1420s]

[72]   https://www.myindiamyglory.com/2017/10/07/maharishi-kanad-discovered-atomic-theory-2600-years-ago-not-dalton/

[73]   https://www.mysteryofindia.com/2014/11/acharya-kanad-the-father-of-atomic-theory.html

[74]   Archimedes to Hawking: Laws of Science and the Great Minds Behind Them By Clifford Pickover

[75]   https://www.mysteryofindia.com/2015/02/law-gravity-discovered-indian.html

[76]   https://www.javatpoint.com/brahmagupta

[77]   Chetan Kumar Sahu, BRAHMAGUPTA: A NAME THAT BROUGHT INDIA'S NAME TO TOP IN MATHEMATICS, International Research Journal of Modernization in Engineering Technology and Science, Volume:03, Issue:10, October-2021

[78]   https://www.encyclopedia.com/people/science-and-technology/astronomy-biographies/brahmagupta

[79]   https://www.myindiamyglory.com/2019/12/18/nagarjuna-wizard-in-alchemy-metallurgy-introduced-gold-shine-mechanism/

[80-81] SCIENTISTS OF ANCIENT INDIA, Chapter 15, Indian Culture and Heritage, pp. 229-235, NIOS, updated on 10.09.2020

[82] https://www.myindiamyglory.com/2019/12/18/nagarjuna-wizard-in-alchemy-metallurgy-introduced-gold-shine-mechanism/

[83] SCIENTISTS OF ANCIENT INDIA, Chapter 15, Indian Culture and Heritage, pp. 229-235, NIOS, updated on 10.09.2020

[84-85] https://prepp.in/news/e-492-sushruta-ancient-india-history-notes

[86] https://www.indiatoday.in/education-today/gk-current-affairs/story/sushruta-works-indian-physician-medicine-plastic-surgery-rhinoplasty-nose-job-1559599-2019-07-01

[87] Sakharkar Bhagyashri, Vithalani Lalitkumar, CONCEPT OF COSMETOLOGY IN ANCIENT INDIA WITH SPECIAL SUSHRUTA SAMHITA, INTERNATIONAL AYURVEDIC MEDICAL JOURNAL, Volume 6, Issue 4, April, 2018

[88] Mukhopadhyay, B & Sharma, Kalu. (1992). Cataract surgery in susruta samhita. Ancient science of life. 11. 169-73.

[89] https://prepp.in/news/e-492-sushruta-ancient-india-history-notes

[90] SCIENTISTS OF ANCIENT INDIA, Chapter 15, Indian Culture and Heritage, pp.229-235, NIOS, updated on 10.09.2020

[91]   https://prepp.in/news/e-492-sushruta-ancient-india-history-notes

[92]   Rajeshwari P. N, Description of Bhagna as per Sushrutha samhitha & contemporary surgical practice (https://iamj.in/SHALYA_TANTRA%20(Surgery)/images/upload/Bhagnaas_per_Sushruta.pdf)

[93]   Sakharkar Bhagyashri, Vithalani Lalitkumar, CONCEPT OF COSMETOLOGY IN ANCIENT INDIA WITH SPECIAL SUSHRUTA SAMHITA, INTERNATIONAL AYURVEDIC MEDICAL JOURNAL, Volume 6, Issue 4, April, 2018

[94]   https://www.indiatoday.in/education-today/gk-current-affairs/story/sushruta-works-indian-physician-medicine-plastic-surgery-rhinoplasty-nose-job-1559599-2019-07-01

[95]   Bagde, Ashvin. (2013), Charak Samhita-Complete Encyclopedia of Ayurvedic Science

[96]   SCIENTISTS OF ANCIENT INDIA, Chapter 15, Indian Culture and Heritage, pp. 229-235, NIOS, updated on 10.09.2020

[97]   https://en.wikipedia.org/wiki/Charaka

[98]   Priyanka Triwedi, GENETICS IN AYURVEDA: VIEW OF ANCIENT SCHOLARS, IAMJ, Volume 4, Issue 08, August- 2016

[99]   SCIENTISTS OF ANCIENT INDIA, Chapter 15, Indian Culture and Heritage, pp. 229-235, NIOS, updated on 10.09.2020

[100] SCIENTISTS OF ANCIENT INDIA, Chapter 15, Indian Culture and Heritage, pp. 229-235, NIOS, updated on 10.09.2020

[101] https://en.wikipedia.org/wiki/Patanjali

[102] https://en.wikipedia.org/wiki/Yoga_Sutras_of_ Patanjali

[103] https://en.wikipedia.org/wiki/Kalidasa

[104] https://en.wikipedia.org/wiki/Shakuntala_(play)

[105] https://360hinduism.com/abhijnanasakuntalam-one-worlds-best-play/

[106] The Raghuvamsa of Kalidasa, KAS'INATHA PANDURANGA PARABA, THE NIRNAYA-SAGARA PRESS, BOMBAY, 1886

[107] https://prepp.in/news/e-492- raghuvamsa-kalidasa-ancient-india- history-notes

[108] https://en.wikipedia.org/wiki/Shudraka

[109] R. K. Jha, Kalpana Rajput, Sudraka: The Mrichchhakatika (Tr. By M. R. Kale)--A Study, Prakash Book Depot, 2020

[110] M. R. Kale, The Mrichchhakatika of Sudraka: With Introduction, Critical Essays and a Photo Essay, 2016, ISBN: 978-8120840102

[111] https://literaryyog.com/mrichchhakatika-the-little-clay-cart-sudraka/

[112] https://prepp.in/news/e-492-mrichchhakatika-the-little-clay-cart-shudaka-ancient-india-history-notes

[113]   Anthony Kennedy Warder, Indian Kāvya Literature,

[114]   Viśvanātha Devaśarmā, Biswanath Banerjee, Shudraka

[115]   https://prepp.in/news/e-492-vinavasavadatta-shudaka-ancient-india-history-notes

[116]   Apparao, Ponangi Sri Rama, Special Aspects of Nāṭya Śāstra, National School of Drama, 2001

[117]   https://en.wikipedia.org/wiki/Vishakhadatta#cite_note-1

[118]   Prof. K. H. Dhruva, Visakhadatta's Mudra-Rakshasa

[119]   https://prepp.in/news/e-492-mudrarakashasa-vishakhadatta-ancient-india-history-notes

[120]   https://www.vedantu.com/question-answer/vishakhadatta-wrote-class-10-social-science-cbse-5fe98c2fa729973d3f92739c

[121]   *Pandey, Ravi Narayan (2007), Encyclopaedia of Indian literature, vol. 1, Anmol Publications,* ISBN 978-81-261-3118-1

[122]   Kosambi, D.D. Combined Methods in Indology (PDF). p. 192, 2005, ISBN: 978-0195677300

[123]   Mirashi, V. V. (1996). "The Mahavira-charita". Bhavabhūti. Motilal Banarsidass Publishers. ISBN 81-208-1180-1

[124]   "Bhavabuti". Dictionary Of Indology. Pustak Mahal. 2009. p. 32

[125] Uttara ramacharita, IN: CLASSICAL SANSKRUT LITERATURE, HINDU SCRIPTURES, INTRODUCTION OF SCRIPTURES

[126] https://www.hinduscriptures.com/hindu-scriptures/uttara-ramacharita/20825/

[127] Warder, Anthony Kennedy, Indian Kavya Literature: The early medieval period (Shudraka to Vishakhadatta), Motilal Banarsidass. p. 75, 1990, ISBN 978-81-208-0448-7.

[128] Sharma, Tej Ram, A Political History of the Imperial Guptas: From Gupta to Skandagupta, Concept Publishing Company. p. 90, 1989, ISBN 978-81-7022-251-4.

[129] Keith, Arthur Berriedale, A History of Sanskrit literature, Oxford University Press, 1966

[130] https://prepp.in/news/e-492-allahabad-pillar-inscription-prayag-prasasti-art-and-culture-notes

[131] *Stoneman, RiFard (2019)*. The Greek Experience of India: From Alexander to the Indo-Greeks. *p. 414.* ISBN 978-0-691-15403-9.

[132] *Varadpande, M. L.; Varadpande, Manohar Laxman (1987)*. History of Indian Theatre. *Abhinav Publications.* ISBN 978-81-7017-221-5

[133] https://www.hinduscriptures.com/hindu-scriptures/svapnavasavadattam-of-bhasa/20817/

[134] Motilal Banarsidass; 7th edition (1 January 2015), ISBN-13: 978-8120805729

[135]   S. K. Sharma (2005), Karnabharam and Madhyama-vyayoga, ISBN: 978-8171102563

[136]   Ramen Goswami (2022), Deception (Chalana) of Karna in Karnabharama by Bhasa, International Journal of Research Publication and Reviews

[137]   https://www.hinduscriptures.com/hindu-scriptures/karnabharam/20792/

[138]   K. Krishnamoorthy (2017), Banabhatta, Sahitya Akademi, New Delhi

[139]   Singh, U. P. (2021). The Bais Kshatriyas; Rise and Decline of a Rajput Dynasty in Northern India. Asian Man (The)-An International Journal, 15(1), 4-21.

[140]   Bana (Author), Padmini Rajappa (Translator), Kadambari: Bana, Penguin India, 2010

[141]   *C. M. Ridding (1896), The Kādambarī of Bāṇa. Translated, with Occasional Omissions, And Accompanied by a Full Ab]ra^ of the Continuation of the Romance by the Author's Son Bhūshaṇabhaṭṭa*

[142]   https://bhagavadgita.org.in/Blogs/5ad06c865369e d119c551fc5

[143]   A. K. Warder (2004), Indian Kāvya literature, Part 1, Motilal Banarsidass Publ., pp. 198–233, ISBN 978-81-208-0445-6

[144]   D. D. (Dhruv Dev). Sharma (2005), Panorama of Indian Anthroponomy, Mittal Publications, p. 117, ISBN 978-81-8324-078-9

[145]   A. K. Warder (2004), Indian Kāvya literature, Part 1, Motilal Banarsidass Publ., p. 225, ISBN 978-81-208-0445-6

[146]   https://www.hindu-blog.com/2012/02/kiratarjuniya-story-of-kirata-shiva-as.html

[147]   Ajanta Caves: Advisory Body Evaluation, UNESCO International Council on Monuments and Sites, 1982, archived 22 December 2009 at the Wayback Machine

[148]   Spink, Walter M. (2007), Ajanta: History and Development, Volume 5: Cave by Cave. Leiden: Brill, ISBN 978-90-04-15644-9

[149]   Ring, Trudy; Salkin, Robert M.; La Boda, Sharon (1994), Asia and Oceania. Routledge, pp. 14–19. ISBN 978-1-884964-04-6

[150]   Schastok, Sara L. (1985), The Śāmalājī Sculptures and 6th Century Art in Western India, Brill Academic, p. 40, ISBN 978-90-04-06941-1

[151]   Spink, Walter M. (2006), Ajanta: History and Development, Volume 2: Arguments about Ajanta, Leiden: Brill, ISBN 978-90-04-15072-0

[152]   Spink, Walter M. (2009), Ajanta: History and Development, Volume 4: Painting, Sculpture, Architecture, Year by Year, Leiden: Brill, ISBN 978-90-04-14983-0

[153]   Cohen, Richard S. (2006a), Beyond Enlightenment: Buddhism, Religion, Modernity, Routledge, ISBN 978-1-134-19205-2

[154]   Spink, Walter M. (2007), Ajanta: History and Development, Volume 5: Cave by Cave. Leiden: Brill, ISBN 978-90-04-15644-9

[155]   Michell, George (2009), The Penguin Guide to the Monuments of India, Volume 1: Buddhist, Jain, Hindu, Penguin Books, ISBN 978-0-14-008144-2

[156]   Susheila Ghosal (2006), SANCHI REDISCOVERED, Magpie Books India Ltd., Faridabad (nd), ISBN 8187363886

[157]   Britannica, The Editors of Encyclopaedia. "Great Stupa". Encyclopedia Britannica, 8 Jan. 2023, https://www.britannica.com/place/Great-Stupa-Buddhist-monument-Sanchi-India. Accessed 24 May 2023.

[158]   https://en.wikipedia.org/wiki/Sanchi

[159]   https://approachguides.com/blog/buddhist-stupa-architecture-symbolism/

[160]   "Ellora Caves". Encyclopedia Britannica, 6 May. 2023, https://www.britannica.com/place/Ellora-Caves. Accessed 26 May 2023.

[161]   "World Heritage Sites - Ellora Caves, Ellora Caves (1983), Maharashtra", Archaeological Survey of India, Archived from the original on 30 March 2014.

[162]   Dhavalikar, Madhukar Keshav (2003), Ellora. Oxford University Press, New Delhi, ISBN 0-19-565458-7

[163]   P. R. Srinivasan (2007), Ellora, Archaeological Survey of India, ISBN 978-81-87780-43-4.

[164] Dhavalikar, Madhukar Keshav (2003), Ellora, Oxford University Press, New Delhi, ISBN 0-19-565458-7

[165] Geri Hockfield Malandra (1993), Unfolding A Mandala: The Buddhist Cave Temples at Ellora, State University of New York Press, ISBN 978-0-7914-1355-5.

[166] "World Heritage Sites – Pattadakal", Archaeological Survey of India, Retrieved 21 June 2016.

[167] World Heritage Sites – Pattadakal– More Detail, Archaeological Survey of India, Government of India (2012)

[168] Kadasiddheswara Temple Archived 1 October 2017, the Wayback Machine, ASI India (2011)

[169] Michell, George (2017), Badami, Aihole, Pattadakal, Jaico (Reprinted, Orig Year: 2011), ISBN 978-81-8495-600-9.

[170] Jambulingeswara Temple Archived 23 March 2018, the Wayback Machine, ASI India (2011)

[171] Michell, George (2017), Badami, Aihole, Pattadakal, Jaico (Reprinted, Orig Year: 2011), ISBN 978-81-8495-600-9.

[172] Michell, George (2017), Badami, Aihole, Pattadakal, Jaico (Reprinted, Orig Year: 2011), ISBN 978-81-8495-600-9.

[173] Chandrashekhara Temple Archived 23 March 2018, the Wayback Machine, ASI India (2011)

[174] Michell, George (2017), Badami, Aihole, Pattadakal, Jaico (Reprinted, Orig Year: 2011), ISBN 978-81-8495-600-9.

[175] Sangameshwara Temple Archived 1 October 2017, the Wayback Machine, ASI India (2011)

[176] Carol Radcliffe Bolon (1985), The Durga Temple, Aihole, and the Saṅgameśvara Temple, KūḌavelli: A Sculptural Review, Ars Orientalis, The Smithsonian Institution and Department of the History of Art, University of Michigan, Vol. 15, pages 47-64

[177] Michell, George (2017), Badami, Aihole, Pattadakal, Jaico (Reprinted, Orig Year: 2011), ISBN 978-81-8495-600-9.

[178] Heather Elgood (2000), Hinduism and the Religious Arts, Bloomsbury Academic, ISBN 978-0-304-70739-3.

[179] Vinayak Bharne, Krupali Krusche (2014), Rediscovering the Hindu Temple: The Sacred Architecture and Urbanism of India. Cambridge Scholars, ISBN 978-1-4438-6734-4.

[180] Norman Yoffee (2007), Negotiating the Past in the Past: Identity, Memory, and Landscape in Archaeological Research, University of Arizona Press, pp. 164–167, ISBN 978-0-8165-2670-3.

[181] Michell, George (2017), Badami, Aihole, Pattadakal, Jaico (Reprinted, Orig Year: 2011), ISBN 978-81-8495-600-9.

[182] Kasivisweswara Temple Archived 22 April 2018, the Wayback Machine, ASI India (2011)

[183] Mallikarjuna Temple Archived 23 February 2017, the Wayback Machine, ASI India (2011)

[184] Michael W. Meister, Madhusudan A. Dhaky (1996), Encyclopaedia of Indian Temple Architecture, American Institute of Indian Studies, ISBN 978-81-86526-00-2.

[185] Michell, George (2017), Badami, Aihole, Pattadakal, Jaico (Reprinted, Orig Year: 2011), ISBN 978-81-8495-600-9.

[186] Blackburn, Stuart (1996), "The Brahmin and the Mongoose: The Narrative Context of a Well-Travelled Tale", Bulletin of the School of Oriental and African Studies, Cambridge University Press, 59 (3): 494–506, doi:10.1017/s0041977x00030615.

[187] Virupaksha Temple Archived 1 November 2017, the Wayback Machine, ASI India (2011)

[188] Munshi, K. M (1954), History And Culture Of The Indian People Vol. 3 (classical Age).

[189] "The Temples of Pattadakal", World History Encyclopedia, Retrieved 27 August 2021.

[190] George Michell (2002), Pattadakal, Oxford University Press, ISBN 978-0-19-565651-0.

[191] Kadambi, Hemanth (2015), "Cathleen Cummings, Decoding a Hindu Temple: Royalty and Religion in the Iconographic Program of the Virupaksha Temple, Pattadakal", South Asian Studies, Taylor & Francis, 31 (2): 266–268, doi:10.1080/02666030.2015.1094214.

[192]   George Michell (1977), The Hindu Temple: An Introduction to Its Meaning and Forms, University of Chicago Press, ISBN 978-0-226-53230-1.

[193]   Stella Kramrisch (1993), The Hindu Temple, Motilal Banarsidass, pp. 241–242 with footnotes, ISBN 978-81-208-0223-0.

[194]   Stella Kramrisch (1993), The Hindu Temple, Motilal Banarsidass, pp. 241–242 with footnotes, ISBN 978-81-208-0223-0.

[195]   Cathleen Cummings (2014), Decoding a Hindu Temple: Royalty and Religion in the Iconographic Program of the Virupaksha Temple, Pattadakal. South Asian Studies, ISBN 978-0-9834472-6-9.

[196]   Lippe, Aschwin (1967), "Some Sculptural Motifs on Early Calukya Temples", Artibus Asiae, 29 (1): 5–24. doi:10.2307/3250288.

[197]   John Stratton Hawley (1987), Krishna and the Birds, Ars Orientalis, The Smithsonian Institution and Department of the History of Art, University of Michigan, Vol. 17, pp. 137-161

[198]   M. K. Dhavalikar (1982), "Kailasa — The Stylistic Development and Chronology", Bulletin of the Deccan College Research Institute. 41: 33–45.

[199]   Papanatha Temple, ASI India (2011)

[200]   Jaina Temple Archived 1 December 2015, the Wayback Machine, ASI India (2011)

[201]   Adam Hardy (1995), Indian Temple Architecture: Form and Transformation: the Karṇāṭa Drāviḍa Tradition, 7th to 13th Centuries, Abhinav, ISBN 978-81-7017-312-0.

www.ingramcontent.com/pod-product-compliance
Lightning Source LLC
Chambersburg PA
CBHW031415150726
47989CB00002B/674